Bloom's BioCritiques

Bloom's BioCritiques

William Blake

Edited and with an introduction by
Harold Bloom
Sterling Professor of the Humanities
Yale University

CHELSEA HOUSE
PUBLISHERS
A Haights Cross Communications Company ®
Philadelphia

Library of Congress Cataloging-in-Publication Data
William Blake / edited and with an introduction by Harold Bloom.
    p. cm. — (Bloom's biocritiques)
  Includes index.
  "Works by William Blake"—P. ...
  "Works about William Blake"— P. ...
  ISBN 0-7910-8571-6
  1. Blake, William,, 1757-1827. 2. Poets, English—18th century—Biography.
3. Poets, English—19th century—Biography. 4. Artists—Great Britain—
Biography. I. Bloom, Harold. II. Series.
  PR4146.W463 2005
  821'.7—dc22

                                        2005008872

Contributing editor: Heather Dubnick
Cover design by Keith Trego
Cover: © Getty Images, Inc.
Layout by EJB Publishing Services

CONTENTS

User's Guide

These volumes are designed to introduce the reader to the life and work of the world's literary masters. Each volume begins with Harold Bloom's essay "The Work in the Writer" and a volume-specific introduction also written by Professor Bloom. Following these unique introductions is an engaging biography that discusses the major life events and important literary accomplishments of the author under consideration.

Furthermore, each volume includes an original critique that not only traces the themes, symbols, and ideas apparent in the author's works, but strives to put those works into a cultural and historical perspective. In addition to the original critique is a brief selection of significant critical essays previously published on the author and his or her works followed by a concise and informative chronology of the writer's life. Finally, each volume concludes with a bibliography of the writer's works, a list of additional readings, and an index of important themes and ideas.

HAROLD BLOOM

The Work in the Writer

Literary biography found its masterpiece in James Boswell's *Life of Samuel Johnson*. Boswell, when he treated Johnson's writings, implicitly commented upon Johnson as found in his work, even as in the great critic's life. Modern instances of literary biography, such as Richard Ellmann's lives of W.B. Yeats, James Joyce, and Oscar Wilde, essentially follow in Boswell's pattern.

That the writer somehow is in the work, we need not doubt, though with William Shakespeare, writer-of-writers, we almost always need to rely upon pure surmise. The exquisite rancidities of the Problem Plays or Dark Comedies seem to express an extraordinary estrangement of Shakespeare from himself. When we read or attend *Troilus and Cressida* and *Measure for Measure*, we may be startled by particular speeches of Ulysses in the first play, or of Vincentio in the second. These speeches, of Ulysses upon hierarchy or upon time, or of Duke Vincentio upon death, are too strong either for their contexts or for the characters of their speakers. The same phenomenon occurs with Parolles, the military impostor of *All's Well That Ends Well*. Utterly disgraced, he nevertheless affirms: "Simply the thing I am / Shall make me live."

In Shakespeare, more even than in his peers, Dante and Cervantes, meaning always starts itself again through excess or overflow. The strongest of Shakespeare's creatures—Falstaff, Hamlet, Iago, Lear, Cleopatra—have an exuberance that is fiercer than their plays can contain. If Ben Jonson was at all correct in his complaint that "Shakespeare wanted art," it could have been only in a sense that he may not have intended. Where do the personalities of Falstaff or Hamlet touch a limit? What was it in Shakespeare that made *Hamlet* and the two parts of *Henry IV* into "plays unlimited"? Neither Falstaff nor Hamlet will be stopped: their wit, their beautiful, laughing speech, their intensity of being—all these are virtually infinite.

In what ways do Falstaff and Hamlet manifest the writer in the work? Evidently, we can never know, or know enough to answer with any authority. But what would happen if we reversed the question, and asked: How did the work form the writer, Shakespeare?

Of Shakespeare's inwardness, his biography tells us nothing. And yet, to an astonishing extent, Shakespeare created our inwardness. At the least, we can speculate that Shakespeare so lived his life as to conceal the depths of his nature, particularly as he rather prematurely aged. We do not have Shakespeare on Shakespeare, as any good reader of the Sonnets comes to realize: they do not constitute a key that unlocks his heart. No sequence of sonnets could be less confessional or more powerfully detached from the poet's self.

The German poet and universal genius, Goethe, affords a superb contrast to Shakespeare. Of Goethe's life, we know more than everything; I wonder sometimes if we know as much about Napoleon or Freud or any other human being who ever has lived, as we know about Goethe. Everywhere, we can find Goethe in his work, so much so that Goethe seems to crowd the writing out, just as Byron and Oscar Wilde seem to usurp their own literary accomplishments. Goethe, cunning beyond measure, nevertheless invested a rival exuberance in his greatest works that could match his personal charisma. The sublime outrageousness of the Second Part of *Faust*, or of the greater lyric and meditative poems, forms a Counter-Sublime to Goethe's own daemonic intensity.

Goethe was fascinated by the daemonic in himself; we can doubt that Shakespeare had any such interests. Evidently, Shakespeare abandoned his acting career just before he composed *Measure for Measure* and *Othello*. I surmise that the egregious interventions by Vincentio and Iago displace the actor's energies into a new kind of mischief-making, a fresh opening to a subtler playwriting-within-the-play.

But what had opened Shakespeare to this new awareness? The answer is the work in the writer, *Hamlet* in Shakespeare. One can go further: it was not so much the play, *Hamlet*, as the character Hamlet, who changed Shakespeare's art forever.

Hamlet's personality is so large and varied that it rivals Goethe's own. Ironically Goethe's Faust, his Hamlet, has no personality at all, and is as colorless as Shakespeare himself seems to have chosen to be. Yet nothing could be more colorful than the Second Part of *Faust*, which is peopled by an astonishing array of monsters, grotesque devils and classical ghosts.

A contrast between Shakespeare and Goethe demonstrates that in each—but in very different ways—we can better find the work in the person, than we can discover that banal entity, the person in the work. Goethe to many of his contemporaries seemed to be a mortal god. Shakespeare, so far as we know, seemed an affable, rather ordinary fellow, who aged early and became somewhat withdrawn. Yet Faust, though Mephistopheles battles for his soul, is hardly worth the trouble unless you take him as an idea and not as a person. Hamlet is nearly every-idea-in-one, but he is precisely a personality and a person.

Would Hamlet be so astonishingly persuasive if his father's ghost did not haunt him? Falstaff is more alive than Prince Hal, who says that the devil haunts him in the shape of an old fat man. Three years before composing the final *Hamlet*, Shakespeare invented Falstaff, who then never ceased to haunt his creator. Falstaff and Hamlet may be said to best represent the work in the writer, because their influence upon Shakespeare was prodigious. W.H. Auden accurately observed that Falstaff possesses infinite energy: never tired, never bored, and absolutely both witty and happy until Hal's rejection destroys him. Hamlet too has infinite energy, but in him it is more curse than blessing.

Falstaff and Hamlet can be said to occupy the roles in Shakespeare's invented world that Sancho Panza and Don Quixote possess in Cervantes's. Shakespeare's plays from 1610 on (starting with *Twelfth Night*) are thus analogous to the Second Part of Cervantes's epic novel. Sancho and the Don overtly jostle Cervantes for authorship in the Second Part, even as Cervantes battles against the impostor who has pirated a continuation of his work. As a dramatist, Shakespeare manifests the work in the writer more indirectly. Falstaff's prose genius is revived in the scapegoating of Malvolio by Maria and Sir Toby Belch, while Falstaff's darker insights are developed by Feste's melancholic wit. Hamlet's intellectual resourcefulness, already deadly, becomes poisonous in Iago and in Edmund. Yet we have not crossed into the deeper abysses of the work in the writer in later Shakespeare.

No fictive character, before or since, is Falstaff's equal in self-trust. Sir John, whose delight in himself is contagious, has total confidence both in his self-awareness and in the resources of his language. Hamlet, whose self is as strong, and whose language is as copious, nevertheless distrusts both the self and language. Later Shakespeare is, as it were, much under the influence both of Falstaff and of Hamlet, but they tug him in opposite directions. Shakespeare's own copiousness of language is well-nigh incredible: a vocabulary in excess of twenty-one thousand words, almost eighteen hundred of which he coined himself. And of his word-hoard, nearly half are used only once each, as though the perfect setting for each had been found, and need not be repeated. Love for language and faith in language are Falstaffian attributes. Hamlet will darken both that love and that faith in Shakespeare, and perhaps the Sonnets can best be read as Falstaff and Hamlet counterpointing against one another.

Can we surmise how aware Shakespeare was of Falstaff and Hamlet, once they had played themselves into existence? *Henry IV, Part I* appeared in six quarto editions during Shakespeare's lifetime; *Hamlet* possibly had four. Falstaff and Hamlet were played again and again at the Globe, but Shakespeare knew also that they were being read, and he must have had contact with some of those readers. What would it have been like to discuss Falstaff or Hamlet with one of their early readers (presumably also part of their audience at the Globe), if you were the creator of such demiurges? The question would seem nonsensical to most Shakespeare scholars, but then these days they tend to be either ideologues or moldy figs. How can we recover the uncanniness of Falstaff and of Hamlet, when they now have become so familiar?

A writer's influence upon himself is an unexplored problem in criticism, but such an influence is never free from anxieties. The biocritical problem (which this series attempts to explore) can be divided into two areas, difficult to disengage fully. Accomplished works affect the author's life, and also affect her subsequent writings. It is simpler for me to surmise the effect of *Mrs. Dalloway* and *To the Lighthouse* upon Woolf's late *Between the Acts*, than it is to relate Clarissa Dalloway's suicide and Lily Briscoe's capable endurance in art to the tragic death and complex life of Virginia Woolf.

There are writers whose lives were so vivid that they seem sometimes to obscure the literary achievement: Byron, Wilde, Malraux, Hemingway. But most major Western writers do not live that exuberantly, and the greatest of all, Shakespeare, sometimes appears to have adopted the personal mask of colorlessness. And yet there are heroes of literature who struggled titanically with their own eras—Tolstoy, Milton, Victor Hugo—who nevertheless matter more for their works than their lives.

There are great figures—Emily Dickinson, Wallace Stevens, Willa Cather—who seem to have had so little of the full intensity of life when compared to the vitality of their work, that we might almost speak of the work in the work, rather than even of the work in a person. Emily Brontë might well be the extreme instance of such a visionary, surpassing William Blake in that one regard.

I conclude this general introduction to a series of literary bio-critiques by stating a tentative formula or principle for gauging the many ways in which the work influences the person and her subsequent, later work. Our influence upon ourselves is always related to the Shakespearean invention of self-overhearing, which I have written about in several other contexts. Life, as well as poetry and prose, is overheard rather than simply heard. The writer listens to herself as though she were somebody else, and the will to change begins to operate. The forces that live in us include the prior work we have done, and the dreams and waking visions that evade our dismissals.

HAROLD BLOOM

Introduction

What happens to a poem after it has succeeded in clearing a space for
itself? As the poem itself begins to be misread, both by other poems and
by criticism, is it distorted in the same way or differently than it has been
distorted by itself, through its own activity in misreading others? Clearly
its meanings do change drastically between the time that it first wrestles
its way into strength, and the later time that follows its canonization.
What kinds of misreading does canonization bring about? Or, to start
further back, why call the canonization of texts a necessary misreading of
texts?

What is canonization, in a purely secular context, and why ought
criticism to talk about it? Criticism in fact hardly has talked about canon-
formation, at least for quite a while now, and the process is a
troublesome one, and so not easy to discuss. Canon-formation, in the
West, began in the creation of Scripture, when the rabbis accepted
certain texts and rejected others, so as to arrive at last at the library of
thirty-nine books now commonly referred to as the Old Testament. The
rabbis were no more unanimous than any other body of literary critics,
and some of the disputes about canonization were not settled for several
generations. The three main divisions of the Hebrew Bible—the Law,
the Prophets, the Writings or Wisdom literature—represent three
stages of canon-formation. It is likely that the Law was canonized by
about 400 B.C., the Prophets by about 100 B.C., the Writings not until
A.D. 90.

"Canon" as a word goes back to a Greek word for a measuring rule, which in Latin acquired the additional meaning of "model." In English we use it to mean a church code, a secular law, a standard or criterion, or a part of the Catholic Mass, or as a musical synonym for a kind of fugue, or in printing for a size of type. But we also use it for authoritative lists of works, sacred or secular, by one author or by many. The Greek word *kanon* was of Semitic origin, and it is difficult to distinguish between its original meanings of "reed" or "pipe," and "measuring rod." Canon-formation or canonization is a richly suggestive word for a process of classic-formation in poetic tradition, because it associates notions of music and of standards.

But before considering poetic canon-formation, I want to go back to the biblical process of canonization. Samuel Sandmel makes the useful observation that before a text was canonized, it could be copied with inattention, as you or I tend to copy. But, he adds: "Once a writing became canonical, it was copied with such relentless fidelity that even the inherited mistakes and the omissions and the telescoping were retained." The late Edmund Wilson, perhaps not understanding the indirect descent of academic textual scholars from these pious copyists, complained bitterly at its modern continuance, but we can attain a critical realization about how a copying-canonization fosters misreading, of a peculiarly uninteresting, weak, and unproductive kind. A canonical reading, like a canonical copying, attempts to stop the mind by making a text redundantly identical with itself, so as to produce a total presence, an unalterable meaning. So many texts, so many meanings—might be the motto of weak canonization. But there is also strong canonization, and it is more dangerous, whether carried on by the Academy of Ezra, the Church, the universities, or most of all by strong critics from Dr. Samuel Johnson to the present day. Though my own texts-for-reading in this [essay] will be two famous lyrics by Blake, *London* and *The Tyger*, I will try to illustrate the ways in which strong canonization misreads by a religious example, before I turn to Blake. But before I come to my religious example, I want to say something about the transition from religious to secular canon-formation.

Whether in religion or in poetry, or (as I suspect) everywhere else as well, memory is a crucial mode of thought, as Hannah Arendt remarks in the context of political philosophy. We can make a more drastic assertion; in poetry memory is always the most important mode of thought, despite Blake's passionate insistences upon the contrary view. The reason why most strong post-Enlightenment poems end with schemes of transumption or metaleptic reversals, with defensive patterns of projection and/or introjection, with imagery of earliness and/or belatedness, in short with the revisionary ratio I have called the *apophrades* or Return of the Dead, is that, particularly in poems, the past, like the future, is always a force, and indeed, in poems, the future's force is directed to driving the poem back into the past, no matter what the poet is trying to do.

Hannah Arendt tells us that political thought as a tradition goes from Plato to Marx, and ends there. I suppose we could say that moral psychology as a tradition goes from Plato to Freud and ends there. But poetry as a tradition has no Marx or Freud (though Wordsworth came closest to that end-stop position) because you cannot break the tradition without ceasing to write poetry, in the sense that the tradition from Homer to Goethe defines poetry, and Wordsworth's best poetry paradoxically breaks the tradition only to extend it, but at the high cost of narrowing and internalizing the tradition, so that all subsequent attempts to get beyond Wordsworth have failed. Blake was a much less original poet than Wordsworth, as I think we are only beginning to understand. Despite his surface innovations, Blake is closer to Spenser and to Milton than he is to Wordsworth, and far closer than Wordsworth is to Spenser and Milton. Wordsworth imposed himself upon the canon; Blake, though a major intellectual revisionist, was more imposed upon *by* the canon than modern Blake scholarship is willing to accept or admit.

I return to the process of canonic imposition. E.R. Curtius sums it up by saying: "Canon formation in literature must always proceed to a selection of classics." But Curtius, so far as I can tell, hardly distinguishes between religious and secular canon-formation. A secular tradition presumably is open to intruders of genius, rather more readily than a religious tradition, and surely this difference is the crucial one between revisionism and heresy. Revisionism alters *stance*; heresy alters *balance*. A secular canon stands differently, after it subsumes a great revisionist, as British poetry manifested a different relation between the poet and the poem, after Wordsworth. But a religious canon is thrown out of balance by a great heretic, and cannot subsume him unless it is willing to be a different religion, as Lutheranism and Calvinism were very different religions from Catholicism. Joachim of Flora or Eckhart could not become canonical texts, but in the secular canon Blake has been legitimatized. What this has done to Blake is now my concern, a concern I want to illuminate first by one large instance of the reading peculiarities brought about through religious canonization. The book *Koheleth* or Ecclesiastes is, rather astonishingly, a canonical work, part of Scripture. The book Ecclesiasticus, or *The Wisdom of Jesus the Son of Sirach*, was not taken into the canon, and is part of the Old Testament Apocrypha.

As literary works, they both are magnificent; in the King James version, it would be difficult to choose between them for rhetorical power, but Ecclesiastes is far stronger in the original. Their peculiar fascination for my purposes is that they exist in a relation of precursor and ephebe, with Koheleth or Ecclesiastes, written about 250 B.C., being the clearly dominant influence upon Ben Sirach or Ecclesiasticus, written about 200 B.C. By a splendid irony, the canonical Koheleth is a highly problematic text in regard to normative Judaism, while the uncanonical Ben Sirach is explicitly and unquestionably orthodox, a monument to normative Judaism.

Koheleth derives from the Hebrew word *kahal*, meaning "the community" or "the congregation." The Greek "Ecclesiastes," meaning a member of the *ecclesia* or assembly of citizens, is not a very exact equivalent. Neither word, Hebrew or Greek, means "the Preacher," which is a famous mistranslation for Koheleth. Tradition identifies Koheleth with Solomon, a beautiful but false idea. Like his imitator Ben Sirach, Koheleth worked in the literary genre of Wisdom Literature, a vast genre in the ancient Near East. "Instruction" is a synonym for "Wisdom" in this sense, and may be a better modern translation for *Hokmah*, which really meant: "How to live, what to do," but was also used as a synonym for poetry and song, which were not distinguished from Instruction.

Robert Gordis, in the most widely accepted modern study of Koheleth, shows that Koheleth was a teacher in one of the Wisdom academies in third-century B.C. Jerusalem, teaching aristocratic youths, in a quasi-secular way. His ambiance was anything but prophetic, and his highly individual vision of life and religion was much closer to what we would call skeptical humanism than it was to the central traditions of Judaism. God, for Koheleth, is the Being who made us and rules over us, but Koheleth has nothing more to say about Him. God is there at our beginning and at our end; in between what matters is our happiness. How did *this* book become canonized?

Not without a struggle, is part of the answer. The two great interpretative schools of the rabbis Hillel and Shammai fought a long spiritual war over Koheleth, and the Hillelites did not win a final victory until A.D. 90 when the Council of Jamnia (Jabneh) closed out Scripture by affirming that Koheleth was part of the canon. The school of Shammai sensibly asserted that the book was self-contradictory, merely literary, not inspired by God, and was marked plainly by skepticism towards the Torah. The Hillelites insisted that the book was by Solomon (though surely even they knew this was a pious fiction), and pointed to certain passages in the book that were traditionally Torah-oriented. What was the motive of the Hillelites? Theologically, they were liberals, and presumably Koheleth helped them to achieve more daring and open interpretations of the Law. Yet the deeper motive, as with the great Rabbi Akiba's passion for the *Song of Songs*, seems to have been what we call literary or aesthetic esteem. Koheleth was, rhetorically and conceptually, too good a book to lose. Though both a belated and an audacious work, it was taken permanently into Scripture. I myself am a mere amateur at biblical scholarship, yet I want to go further in expressing the misreading of this canonization, for as I read it, Koheleth is a revisionist poem, a strong misprision of Torah, which suffered the happy irony of being absorbed by the precursor against whom it had rebelled, however ambivalently. Koheleth 3:14 echoes Deuteronomy 4:2 and 13:1 in a revisionist way, so as to change the emphasis from the Law's splendor to human powerlessness. It echoes passages in Kings, Samuel, and Leviticus, so as to undo the moral point from a categorical insistence upon righteousness as a divine commandment to the skeptical view that moral error is inevitable and even necessary, but that righteousness is always more humanly sensible if only you can achieve it. Robert Gordis insightfully remarks that Koheleth refers only to Torah and to Wisdom Scripture, and wholly ignores the canonical prophets, as nothing could be more antithetical to his own vision than Isaiah and Ezekiel.

Let us contrast to Koheleth his eloquent and more traditionally pious ephebe Ben Sirach, who about a half-century later seems to have followed much the same profession, teaching pragmatic Wisdom, of a literary kind, at an upper-class academy in Jerusalem. Ben Sirach can be described as the Lionel Trilling of his day, even as his precursor, Koheleth, seems a figure not wholly unlike Walter Pater or even Matthew Arnold, in Arnold's more skeptical moments, though I hasten to add that Arnold was hardly in Koheleth's class as poet or intellect. Ben

Sirach, by a charming but not unexpected antithetical irony, echoes or alludes constantly to Koheleth, but always canonically misreading Koheleth into a Shammai-like high Pharisaic orthodoxy. Wherever Koheleth urges the necessity of pleasure, Ben Sirach invokes the principle of echoing Koheleth while urging restraint, but in the vocabulary of his precursor. Robert Gordis observes that wherever Koheleth is literal in his meaning, Ben Sirach interprets him as being figurative. Any close comparison of the texts of Ecclesiastes and Ecclesiasticus will confirm the analysis that Gordis makes.

Let me sum up this rather intricate excursus upon Koheleth and the book of Jesus Ben Sirach. The revisionist work, through canonization, is misread by being overfigurated by the canonically informed reader. The derivative, orthodox work, left uncanonized because of its belatedness, is misread by being overliteralized by those who come after it, ourselves included.

I turn to two texts of Blake, two famous *Songs of Experience: London* and *The Tyger*. How are we to read these two revisionist lyrics that Blake intended us to canonize, that indeed now are part of the canon of British poetry? What kinds of misreadings are these poems now certain to demand? *London* is a revisionist text with regard to the book of the prophet Ezekiel; *The Tyger* is a revisionist text with regard to the Book of Job, and also in relation to *Paradise Lost*.

Here is the precursor-text for Blake's *London*, chapter 9 of the Book of Ezekiel:

> He cried also in mine ears with a loud voice, saying, "Cause them that have charge over the city to draw near, even every man with his destroying weapon in his hand."
>
> And, behold, six men came from the way of the higher gate, which lieth toward the north, and every man a slaughter weapon in his hand; and one man among them was clothed with linen, with a writer's inkhorn by his side: and they went in, and stood beside the brasen altar.
>
> And the glory of the God of Israel was gone up from the cherub, whereupon he was, to the threshold of the house. And he called to the man clothed with linen, which had the writer's inkhorn by his side;
>
> And the Lord said unto him, "Go through the midst of the city, through the midst of Jerusalem, and set a mark upon the

foreheads of the men that sigh and that cry for all the abominations that be done in the midst thereof."

And to the others he said in mine hearing, "Go ye after him through the city, and smite: let not your eye spare, neither have ye pity: Slay utterly old and young, both maids, and little children, and women: but come not near any man upon whom is the mark; and begin at my sanctuary." Then they began at the ancient men which were before the house.

And he said unto them, "Defile the house, and fill the courts with the slain: go ye forth." And they went forth, and slew in the city.

And it came to pass, while they were slaying them, and I was left, that I fell upon my face, and cried, and said, "Ah Lord God! wilt thou destroy all the residue of Israel in thy pouring out of thy fury upon Jerusalem?"

Then said he unto me, "The iniquity of the house of Israel and Judah is exceeding great, and the land is full of blood, and the city full of perverseness: for they say, 'The Lord hath forsaken the earth, and the Lord seeth not.'

"And as for me also, mine eye shall not spare, neither will I have pity, but I will recompense their way upon their head."

And, behold, the man clothed with linen, which had the inkhorn by his side, reported the matter, saying, "I have done as thou hast commanded me."

Chapter 8 of Ezekiel ends with God's warning that he will punish the people of Jerusalem for their sins. Chapter 9 is Ezekiel's prophetic vision of the punishment being carried out, despite the prophet's attempt at intercession on behalf of a saving remnant. The crucial verse for Blake's *London* is clearly the fourth one, which gives Blake not only the central image of his poem but even the rhyme of "cry" and "sigh":

... And he called to the man clothed with linen, which had the writer's inkhorn by his side;

And the Lord said unto him: "Go through the midst of the city, through the midst of Jerusalem, and set a mark upon the foreheads of the men that sigh and that cry for all the abominations that be done in the midst thereof."

This mark is given to the saving remnant of Jerusalem, who alone are to be spared destruction. The Hebrew word for "mark" used here is *taw*, which is the name also of the letter *t*, the last letter of the Hebrew alphabet, even as zed (*z*) is last in ours, or omega is last in the Greek alphabet. Traditional commentary on Ezekiel interpreted this to mean that the taw set upon the forehead of the righteous would be written in ink and signify *tichyeh*, "you shall live," but the *taw* upon the forehead of the wicked would be written in blood and would signify *tamuth*, "you shall die."

The intertextual relationship between Ezekiel and Blake here is quite unmistakable, even though it also has been quite unnoticed, except by myself, in my role as what Blake denounced as a "Satan's Watch-Fiend." How is Blake revising Ezekiel?

Not, so far as I can tell, by his initial equation of London = Jerusalem, which means that from the start all received readings of this poem, including my own, are wholly mistaken in seeing Blake's poem primarily as a protest against repression, whether societal or individual. That is, all received readings have said or intimated that in the poem *London* Blake presents himself as a prophet or prophetic figure, akin to Ezekiel, with the people of London only roughly akin to those of Ezekiel's Jerusalem, in that they are shown as suffering beneath the counterrevolutionary oppression of the regime of William Pitt. On this view the people, however culpable for weakness or lack of will, are the righteous, and only the State and State Church of Pitt are the wicked. From this, a number of other interpretations necessarily follow throughout the poem, down to the famous lines about the harlot and the new-born infant at the poem's close.

I shall demonstrate, with the aid of what I call "antithetical criticism," that all such interpretations are weak, unproductive, canonical misreadings, quite alien to the spirit of Blake's strong misreading or misprision of Ezekiel, and alien in any case to the letter of Blake's text, to the words, images, figurations of the strong poem *London*.

Blake begins: "I wander thro' each charter'd street," and so we begin also, with that wandering and that chartering, in order to define that "L" Is it an Ezekiel-like prophet, or someone whose role and function are altogether different? To "wander" is to have no destination and no purpose. A biblical prophet may wander when he is cast out into the desert, when his voice becomes a voice in the wilderness, but he does not wander when he goes through the midst of the city, through the midst of Jerusalem the City of God. There, his inspired voice always has purpose, and his inspired feet always have destination. Blake knew all this, and knew it with a knowing beyond our knowing. When he begins by saying that he *wanders* in London, his Jerusalem, his City of God, then he begins also by saying "I am not Ezekiel, I am not a prophet, I am too fearful to be the prophet I ought to be, *I am hid*."

"Charter'd" is as crucial as "wander." The word is even richer with multiple significations and rhetorical ironies, in this context, than criticism so far has noticed. Here are the relevant shades-of-meaning: There is certainly a reference to London having been created originally as a city by a charter to that effect. As certainly, there is an ironic allusion to the celebrated political slogan: "the chartered rights of Englishmen." More subtly, as we will see, there is a reference to *writing*, because to be chartered is to be written, since a charter is a written grant from authority, or a document outlining a process of incorporation. In addition, there are the commercial notions of hiring, or leasing, indeed of binding or covenanting, always crucial in a prophetic context. Most important, I think, in this poem that turns upon a mark of salvation or destruction, is the accepted meaning that to be chartered is to be awarded a special privilege or a particular immunity, which is established by a written document. Finally, there is a meaning opposed to "wandering," which is charting or mapping, so as to preclude mere wandering. The streets of London are chartered, Blake says, and so he adds is the Thames, and we can surmise that for Blake, the adjective is primarily negative in its ironies, since his manuscript drafts show that he substituted the word "chartered" for the word "dirty" in both instances.

As is often the case with strong, antithetical poems that are highly condensed in their language, Blake's key-words in *London* are remarkably interrelated, as criticism again has failed to notice. Walter Pater, in his great essay on *Style*, urges that the strong poet, or "literary artist" as he puts it, "will be apt to restore not really obsolete or really worn-out words, but the finer edge of words still in use." Pater meant the restoration of etymological or original meaning, "the finer edge," and in this Pater was again a prophet of modern or belated poetry. But here Blake, who deeply influenced Pater, was already a pioneer. Let us return to "wander" which goes back to the root *wendh*, from which come also "turn," "weave," and "wind." I quote from Blake's *Auguries of Innocence*, notebook jottings clearly related to his *London*:

The Whore & Gambler by the State
Licencd build that Nations Fate
The Harlots cry from Street to Street
Shall weave Old Englands winding Sheet
The Winners Shout the Losers Curse
Dance before dead Englands Hearse
Every Night & every Morn
Some to Misery are Born

Contrast this to the final stanza of *London*:

But most thro' midnight streets I hear
How the youthful Harlots curse
Blasts the new-born Infants tear
And blights with plagues the Marriage hearse.

The harlot's cry or curse, a loser's curse, weaves a winding sheet for England and every marriage in England by blasting the infant's tear and by blighting with plagues. To weave is to wind is to wander is to turn is to blight and blast. Blight and blast what and how? The surprising answer is: voice, which of course is the prophet's one gift. Blake *wendhs* as the harlot *wendhs*, and both to the same result: the loss of human voice. For what is an "infant"? "Infant," "ban," and "prophet" all come from the same root, the Indo-European *Bha*, which is a root meaning "to speak." And "infant" means one incapable of speech; all the infant can do is weep. The Latin *fari* and the Greek *phanai* both mean "to speak," and "prophet" derives from them. A ban is a stated or spoken interdiction, which means that a ban is a curse, while to curse is to put something or someone under a ban. Ban and voice, in Blake's *London*, are natural synonyms and indeed we can say that the poem offers the following equation: every voice = a ban = a curse = weeping or a blasted tear. But the verbal network is even more intricate. The harlot's curse is not, as various interpreters have said, venereal disease, but is indeed what "curse" came to mean in the vernacular after Blake and still means now: menstruation, the natural cycle in the human female. Let us note the complexity of two more key words in the text: "mark" and "forg'd" in "mind-forg'd manacles." A "mark" is a boundary (or, as Blake said, a "Devourer" as opposed to a "Prolific"); it is also a visible trace, a sign in lieu of writing, and a grade of merit or demerit. To "forge" means to "fabricate" in both senses of "fabricate": to make, as a smith or poet makes, but also to counterfeit. The Indo-European root is *dhabh*, meaning "to fit together" and is related to the Hebrew *dabhar* for "word." "Mind-forg'd manacles" is a phrase deliberately evoking the Western metaphysical problem of dualism, since "manacles" for "hand-cuffs" involves *manus* or hand, and hence bodily act, which is at once made and yet feigned or counterfeited by the opposing principle of mind.

I have involved us in all of this verbal interrelation in order to suggest that Blake's *London* centers itself upon an opposition between *voice* and *writing*, by which I don't mean that somehow Jacques Derrida wrote the poem. No—the poem is precisely anti-Nietzschean, anti-Derridaean, and offers us a terrifying nostalgia for a lost prophetic *voice*, the voice of Ezekiel and religious logocentrism, which has been replaced by a demonic *visible trace*, by a mark, by the writing of the apocalyptic letter *taw*. With this as background, I am at last prepared to offer my own, antithetical, strong misreading of Blake's *London*, of which I will assert only that it is more adequate to the text than the weak misreadings now available to us.

I will commence by offering a very plain summary or paraphrase of what I judge to be the difference in meanings when we juxtapose Blake's *London* with its precursor-text in Ezekiel, chapter 9. Then I will proceed to an antithetical account of Blake's *London*, through a charting of its revisionary ratios, tropes, psychic defenses, and images.

In chapter 8 of Ezekiel, the prophet sits in his house of exile in Babylon, surrounded by the elders of Judah. The Spirit of God raises him, and carries him "in the visions of God to Jerusalem," to the outraged Temple, where graven, idolatrous images of Asherah have been placed as substitutes for the Living God. A further and final vision of the *Merkabah*, God's triumphal chariot, is granted Ezekiel, after which four scenes of idolatry *within* the Temple are revealed to him. Chapter 8 concludes with a fierce warning from God:

> Therefore will I also deal in fury; Mine eye shall not spare, neither will I have pity; and though they cry in Mine ears with a loud voice, yet will I not hear them.

Chapter 9, which I have quoted already, mitigates this only for a small remnant. There are six angels of destruction, with only Gabriel (according to the Talmud) armed with the inkhorn that will spare the righteous. Unlike Gabriel, Blake does not necessarily set a mark, since his "mark in every face I meet," primarily is intransitive, meaning "remark" or "observe."

Blake begins *London* with a curious irony, more a scheme than a figure, or if a figure, then more a figure of thought than of speech. For he adopts the outcast role he called Rintrah, the John-the-Baptist or unheeded forerunner, in place of the prophetic vocation, but in the context of Ezekiel's Jerusalem as well as his own London. In the opening dialectic of presence and absence, precisely what is absent is prophetic direction and prophetic purpose; what is present are chartering and marks. So voice is absent, and only demonic writing is present. Blake's defensive reaction-formation to the call he cannot answer is to be a wanderer, and to mark passively rather than mark actively with the *taws* of righteousness and wickedness, life and death. But righteousness and wickedness are alike absent; present only are weakness and woe, neither of which merits a *taw*, whether of ink or of blood. The synecdoche of the universal human face represents Blake's turning against his own self, for he also is weak and woeful, and not the Ezekiel-like prophet he should be.

The litany of "every" becomes a weird metonymic reification, a regression in moving all men back to a state of infancy, but also an isolation, as this is an "every" that separates out rather than unifies people:

> In every cry of every Man,
> In every Infants cry of fear
> In every voice: in every ban
> The mind-forg'd manacles I hear.

"Every Man" includes the Londoner William Blake, whose voice also must betray the clanking sound of "mind-forg'd manacles," where the mind belongs to every man, again including William Blake. An infant's cry of fear is all-too-natural, for the infant is voiceless but for his fear and hunger, which for him is a kind of fear. When the crucial word "voice" enters the poem, it is put into a metonymic, reductive series with "cry of fear" and "ban," with terror and curse, fear and the threat of fear.

When Blake answers this reduction with a Sublime repressive hyperbole, it is governed by the same "I hear," as spoken by a Jonah, a renegade prophet who never does speak in his own poem, but only hears:

> I hear
> How the Chimney-sweepers cry
> Every blackning Church appalls,
> And the hapless Soldiers sigh,
> Runs in blood down Palace walls.

The chimney-sweepers' cry, as in the two Blakean songs of the sweeps, is "Weep, weep," due to the cockney lisp of the children, as they attempt to advertise their labor with a voiced "sweep, sweep." The cry of weep helps blacken further the perpetually blackening Church, possibly draping it in a pall through the mark of *taw* in a black ink, giving it an edge over the royal palace, which receives the bloody *taw* of destruction. The soldier's hapless sigh prefigures the curse of the harlot, as both are losers, in the term from *Auguries of Innocence*. But what about Blake's synaesthesia? How, even in Sublime representation, can you *hear* a Church being draped in a pall, and how can you *hear* a sigh running in blood down palace walls. The answer, I think, is given by our map of misreading. What Blake is repressing into this hyperbolical hearing-seeing is the visionary power of the *nabi*, the Hebrew prophet, and the running of the repressed voice down the repressive walls represents not only the soldier's hapless sigh, but the more powerful hapless sigh of the prophet who has repressed the voice that is great within us.

We come then to the final stanza, the most weakly misread of all. Here is the characteristic Romantic ending that follows a limiting metaphor by a representing transumption:

> But most thro' midnight streets I hear
> How the youthful Harlots curse
> Blasts the new-born Infants tear
> And blights with plagues the Marriage hearse.

I want to reject altogether the customary interpretation that makes "curse" here a variety of venereal infection, and that makes the infant's condition a prenatal blindness. Instead, I want to reaffirm my own earlier interpretation of the Harlot here as Blake's perpetually youthful

Harlot, Nature, not the human female, but the natural element in the human, male or female.

The inside/outside perspectivism here gives us Blake as pent-up voice wandering still at midnight *through* the streets, and through that labyrinth he achieves another synaesthetic hearing-seeing, how another curse or ban or natural fact (menstruation) blasts or scatters another natural fact, the tearlessness of the new-born *infant*. For Blake every natural fact equals every other natural fact. The metalepsis that introjects the future here is one that sees enormous plagues riding along in every marriage coach, blighting life into death, as though every marriage carries the *taw* of destruction. Remember again the doggerel of *Auguries of Innocence*:

> The Harlots cry from street to street
> Shall weave Old Englands winding sheet
> The Winners Shout the Losers Curse
> Dance before dead Englands Hearse

If Old England is dead, then all her marriages are funerals. A cry that weaves a shroud is like a mark of *taw* or a ban chartering weakness and woe. Blake's poem is not a protest, not a prophetic outcry, not a vision of judgment. It is a revisionist's self-condemnation, a Jonah's desperation at *knowing* he is not an Ezekiel. We misread Blake's poem when we regard it as prophecy, and see it as primarily sympathy with the wretched of London, because we have canonized the poem, and because we cannot bear to read a canonical poem as being truly so altogether negative and self-destructive a text.

Even as a revisionist strong poem, Blake's *London* is more a deliberate parody of misprision than it is a revisionist text. Blake's tonal complexities are uncanny, *unheimlich*, here and elsewhere, and like Nietzsche Blake is something of a parodist of world history. There is a grotesque element in *London*, and what we take as Sublime hyperbole is actually more the underthrow of litotes, the characteristic rhetorical figure in grotesque representation. This parody is a clearer strain in Blake's *The Tyger*, which I want to introduce more by way of Nietzsche than by way of its origins in Job and Milton.

Like Nietzsche, and like every other revisionist, Blake desired always to keep origin and aim, source and purpose, as far apart as possible. Nietzsche, if I understand him, believed only in comic or preposterous schemes of transumption, in which a future laughter is introjected and a past tragedy is projected. An aphorism in *Beyond Good and Evil* says that we are

> prepared as was no previous age for a Carnival in the grand style, for laughter and a high-spirited revelry, for transcendental flights of Sublime nonsense and an Aristophanes-like mockery of the universe. Perhaps this is where we shall yet discover the realm of our invention, that realm in which we also still can be original, say as parodists of world history and the clowns of God—perhaps, even if nothing else today has a future, our laughter may yet have a future.

We can observe here that a poem, in this view, must be a parody of a parody, just as a man is a parody of God. But Nietzschean repetition is even more bewildering, for any copy is both a parody of its original, yet also a self-parody. In terms of poetic misprision, this means that any poem is both a misreading of a precursor poem and, more crucially, a misreading of itself. Whether Nietzschean parody is universally applicable I do not know, but it illuminates poems of deliberately cyclic repetition like Blake's *The Tyger* or *The Mental Traveller* or *The Crystal Cabinet*.

Blake's Tyger has a pretty exact analogue in a Nietzschean tiger, a grand deconstructive tiger, in the curious text called *Truth and Falsehood in an Extra-Moral Sense*:

> What indeed does man know about himself? Oh! that he could but once see himself complete, placed as it were in an illuminated glass case! Does not nature keep secret from him most things, even about his body ...? Nature threw away the key; and woe to the fateful curiosity which might be able for a moment to look out and down through a crevice in the chamber of consciousness and discover that man, indifferent to his own ignorance, is resting on the pitiless, the greedy, and insatiable, the murderous, and as it were, hanging in dreams on the back of a tiger. Whence, in the wide world, with this state of affairs, arises the impulse to truth?

Nietzsche's tiger is human mortality; our illusive day-to-day existence rests us, in dreams, as we ride the tiger who will be, who is our own death, a metaphorical embodiment of the unbearable truth that the pleasure-principle and the reality-principle are finally one.

Nietzsche's precursors were Goethe, Schopenhauer, Heine, and Wagner; Blake's were Milton and the Bible. Of all the thirty-nine books of the Old Testament, Job obsessed Blake most. The forerunners of Blake's Tyger are the Leviathan and Behemoth of Job, two horrible beasts who represent the God-ordained tyranny of nature over man, two beasts whose final name is human death, for to Blake nature is death.

God taunts Job by asking him if these great beasts will make a covenant with man? Rashi comments on Behemoth by saying: "prepared for the future," and the apocryphal apocalypses, Enoch and IV Ezra and Baruch, all say that Leviathan and Behemoth are parted only to come together one day, in the judgment, when they will be the food of the Righteous. As God says of Leviathan, if none dare face him, then "Who is able to stand before Me?" Milton brings in the Leviathan (evidently a crocodile in Job) as a whale, but Melville's Moby-Dick is closer to the beasts of Job, and to Blake's Tyger.

At this advanced date, I assert an exemption from having to argue against the usual run of merely trivial misreadings of *The Tyger*. I will oppose my antithetical reading to the received misreading of the earlier Bloom, in books like *The Visionary Company* and *Blake's Apocalypse*, or in the notes to *Romantic Poetry and Prose* in the Oxford Anthology. The fundamental principle for reading *The Tyger* is to realize that this is a dramatic lyric in which William Blake is not, cannot be, the speaker. *The Tyger* is a Sublime or hyperbolical monologue, with little movement in its tropes or images. It is dominated by the single trope of repression, by an unconsciously purposeful forgetting, but this is not Blake's repression. The psychic area in which the whole poem centers is hysteria. What does it mean for a major lyric never to deviate from its own hysterical intensity?

The answer is that Blake, more even than Nietzsche, is a master of creative parody, and he is parodying a kind of greatness that he loves and admires, but vehemently does not wish to join. It is the greatness of William Cowper, and the other poets of the Burkean or Miltonic Sublime in the later eighteenth century. The two dominant images of the poem are both fearful-the burning or fire and the symmetry. Fire is the prime perspectivizing trope in all of Romanticism, as we will see again and again. It stands, most often, for discontinuity or for the possibility of, or desire towards discontinuity. Its opposite, the emblem of repetition or continuity, tends to be the inland sound of moving waters. These identifications may seem purely arbitrary now; I will vindicate them in later chapters.

What are we to make of "symmetry"? Symmetry is a one-to-one ratio, whether on opposite sides of a dividing line, or in relation to a center. A one-to-one ratio means that no revisionism has taken place; there has been no *clinamen*, no catastrophe-creation or breaking-of-the-vessels in the making of the Tyger. Like Leviathan and Behemoth, the Tyger is exactly what his creator meant him to be. But who is his creator? Does this poem set itself, for interpretation, in a relatively orthodox Genesis-Milton context, or in the context of some Gnosis? How fearful is the Tyger's maker? Or is it a canonical misreading that we allow this poem to set itself a genetic context for interpretation, at all?

By common consent of interpreters, *The Tyger* is made up of a series of increasingly rhetorical questions. The model for this series certainly is to be found in the Book of Job, where God confronts Job with crushingly rhetorical questions, all of them reducing to the cruelty of: Where were you, anyway, when I made everything? After all, Job's plea had been "Call Thou, and I will answer" (13:22), and God therefore relies upon a continuous irony as figure-of-thought. But the speaker of *The Tyger* is incapable of deliberate irony; every one of his tropes is, as I have noted already, a hyperbole. What is this profound repression defending against? What furnace is coming up, at last, against the will of this daemonizing speaker?

No speaker could be more determined to insist that origin and aim were the same impulse and the same event. We can surmise that the unconsciously purposeful forgetting of this poem's speaker is precisely that he himself, as an aim or purpose, has been separated irreparably from his point of origin. Confronting the Tyger, who represents his own *daemonic* intensity, the form that is his own force, what Blake would have called Vision or his own Imagination, the dramatic speaker is desperately determined to identify completely the Tyger's aim and purpose with the Tyger's supposedly divine origins.

Yet it is not the speaker's text, but Blake's, and the meaning of the text rises parodistically and even with a wild comedy out of the intertextual juxtapositions between the text itself and texts by Cowper, by Milton, and the text cited from Job.

First Cowper, from Book VI of *The Task*:

The Lord of all, himself through all diffused,
Sustains, and is the life of all that lives.
Nature is but a name for an effect
Whose cause is God. He feeds the secret fire
By which the mighty process is maintained,
Who sleeps not, is not weary; in whose sight
Slow circling ages are as transient days,
Whose work is without labour; whose designs
No flaw deforms, no difficulty thwarts;

Here origin and purpose are one, without strain, anxiety, or repression, or so it seems. Next Milton, from Book VII of *Paradise Lost*, part of the most Sublime creation-scene in the language:

The grassy Clods now Calv'd, now half appear'd
The Tawny Lion, pawing to get free
His hinder parts, then springs as broke from Bonds,
And Rampant shakes his Brinded mane; the Ounce,
The Libbard, and the Tiger, as the Mole
Rising, the crumbl'd Earth above them threw
In Hillocks ...

Milton shows rather less creative anxiety than the poet of Job, even allowing himself a transumption of a Lucretian allusion as if to indicate his own corrective confidence that God's origins and Milton's purposes are one and the same. Blake's speaker is not Blake, nor is he Milton, not even Blake's own Milton. He is Cowper or Job, or rather Cowper assimilated to Job, and both assimilated not to the strong poet or revisionist in Blake, but to Blake's own Spectre of Urthona, that is, the time-bound work-a-day ego, and not what Blake liked to call "the Real Man the Imagination."

I approach an antithetical formula. Blake's revisionism in *London* was to measure the ratios by which he fell short of Ezekiel. Blake's revisionism in *The Tyger* is to measure the ratio by which he surpasses Cowper and Job. Cowper's fearful ratio does not frighten Blake, whose entire dialectic depends upon separating origins, natural or natural religion's, from imaginative aims or revisionist purposes. Yet, in *London*,

Blake shows himself knowingly incapable of separating prophetic voice as aim or purpose from the cry, curse, ban of natural voice as origin. We have underestimated Blake's complexities, and his own capacity for self-recognition. He is in no danger of falling into the repetition of the Bard confronting the Jobean Tyger. Yet, in the societal context in which a prophet must vindicate himself, Blake falls silent, and falls into the repetition of the wanderer who flees the burden of prophecy. There can no more be a mute prophet than there can be a mute, inglorious Milton. The prophet or *nabi* is precisely a *public orator*, and not a private mutterer or marker. The *nabi* never moans, as Blake did, "I am hid." Blake, who might have been more, by his own account was human—all too human—and gave in to natural fear. His belatedness, in the spiritual more than in the poetic sense, was a shadow that overcame him.

The Blake of *London* has become a canonical writer, unlike the Ben Sirach of Ecclesiasticus, but like Ecclesiasticus Blake gives us in *London* a text he lacks the authority to sustain. The Blake of *The Tyger*, like the Koheleth of Ecclesiastes, gives us a canonical text that tradition necessarily has misread and goes on misreading. Revisionism or belated creations is a hard task, and exacts a very high price, a price that meaning itself must pay for, by being emptied out from a plenitude to a dearth.

I conclude with a final juxtaposition between the skeptical Koheleth and the passionately certain Blake. Both Ecclesiastes and *The Tyger* are texts of conscious belatedness, though *The Tyger* parodies and mocks its own condition of belatedness. For the Tyger itself, as a Sublime representation, is a self-imposed blocking agent, what Blake called a Spectre, and what Ezekiel and Blake called a Covering Cherub. The guilt suffered by the speaker of Blake's *Tyger* is also Cowper's guilt, and the guilt of a very un-Cowperian figure, Milton's Satan. This is the guilt that Nietzsche, in his *Genealogy of Morals*, called the "guilt of indebtedness." I think that Blake meant something like this when he said in *Jerusalem* that it was easier to forgive an enemy than it was to forgive a friend. The speaker of *The Tyger* confronts a burning, fearful symmetry that exists in a one-to-one ratio with its Creator. Like Job confronting Leviathan and Behemoth, the Cowper-like bard confronts an unacceptable surrogate for the divine Precursor, a surrogate who grants him no priority, and who has authority over him insofar as he is natural. Blake, in mocking a canonical kind of poem, nevertheless is subsumed by the canonical traditions of misreading, as any student of *The Tyger*'s interpretative history could testify.

Where Blake's dramatic speaker is trapped in repetition, Koheleth is a theorist of repetition, not far in spirit from the Stoic Marcus Aurelius. "All words toil to weariness," Koheleth says early on in his book, and so he thinks that fundamentally all the books have been written already. Though he praises wisdom, Koheleth is weary of it. He too might have said: "The flesh is sad alas, and I have read all the books." But he adds: "For wisdom is a defense, even as money is a defense," and the Hebrew translated here in the King James version as "defense" is a word literally meaning "shadow." I end on that identification of the defense against influence with the metonymic trope of shade for wisdom or money, and for the forests of the night that frame the menace of the fire that meant a discontinuity from origins.

NEIL HEIMS

Biography of William Blake

They told me that the night & day were all that I could see;
They told me that I had five senses to inclose me up.
And they inclos'd my infinite brain into a narrow circle.
And sunk my heart into the Abyss.
—WILLIAM BLAKE (A., 172)

He was a man without a mask; his aim was single, his path
straight-forwards, and his wants few.
—SAMUEL PALMER in a letter to Alexander Gilchrist

MATTER AND SPIRIT

During his apprenticeship to the engraver, James Basire, young William
Blake was sent to Westminster Abbey to make drawings of the tombs for
engravings Basire had been commissioned to produce for the first
volume of Richard Gough's *Sepulchural Monuments in Great Britain*. The
fifteen year old Blake's task was to do drawings of the royal tombs in the
chapel of St. Edward the Confessor. Blake had to clamber over the
monuments, climb on scaffolding, and even stand on tombs in order to
get full and close views of ornamental representations and the carved
figures of the dead. (Ackroyd 53) On May 2, 1774, he got an even closer
view of mortality when a group of antiquaries gathered in the Abbey to
inspect the condition of the body as the tomb of Edward I was unsealed

and his coffin opened. Blake was there, and not only sketched the four-hundred fifty year old corpse in its coffin, but described its decomposition, starting with the face, which

> was of a dark-brown, or chocolate colour, approaching to black; and so were the hands and fingers. The chin and lips were intire, but without any beard ... Both the lips were prominent; the nose short, as if shrunk; but the apertures of the nostrils were visible ... some globular substance, possibly the flesh part of the eye-balls, was moveable in their sockets under the envelope. Below the chin and under-jaw was lodged a quantity of black dust, which had neither smell nor coherence; but whether the same had been flesh, or spices, could not be ascertained. (Ackroyd 55)

Having such first hand experience of its evanescence, it is not surprising that it was not in corporal reality that Blake sought the incorruptible eternal. Blake believed *that* dwelt in the spiritual, and the spiritual made itself known to Blake through his visions. In Westminster Abbey, for example, "The aisles and galleries of the old cathedral suddenly filled with a great procession of monks and priests, choristers and censer bearers." (Ackroyd 55) These were spirits which appeared to Blake in a vision inside the church. They became processional figures in a drawing he made at the time, too. That things were apprehended in a vision did not diminish their authenticity or actuality. On the contrary, Blake held that visionary experience had more authority than scientifically measurable and verifiable experience. The universe that Sir Isaac Newton was discovering, in Blake's view, was an insulting fiction: "The Indefinite which [is] measure[d] by Newton's Doctrine of the Fluxion of an Atom, A Thing that does not Exist." (Ackroyd 194) The universe according to Blake was not the objective outside which ran by laws, as it was for Newton and Sir Francis Bacon before him, but an internally perceived subjectivity which projected itself, through the agency of the material world, in vision. Eternal reality is, Blake asserted, a spiritual substance made manifest through the accidents of the material world, which vary according to the character of their perceiver, but the eternal, in itself and independent of human interpretation is immutable: "as one age falls, another rises, different to mortal sight, but to immortals only the same.... nothing new occurs in identical existence; Accident ever varies, Substance can never suffer change nor decay." (Ackroyd 287) Of Bacon and Locke, Blake wrote, "They mock Inspiration & Vision. Inspiration & Vision was then & now is & I hope will always Remain my Element my Eternal Dwelling place." (Ackroyd 59)

Blake was not deluded about the nature of his visions. He was aware that they were the fruit of his imagination. One day at a social gathering Blake was asked where he saw a particular vision he had just then described. "Here, madam," he responded indicating his head with his index finger. (Lister 163) By "imagination," however, Blake did not mean the word as it is now commonly used: pretending that something that does not exist does; rather he understood "imagination" to signify the faculty which sees what the eye unaided by it cannot see: the eternal invisible things, the real substance of the spiritual. It is the faculty that transforms invisible reality into images.

The corruptibility of the flesh and the luminosity of his visions led Blake to see our present condition as creatures living upon the earth as an episode in eternity, which must be endured. Our only real joy occurs when we approach the sensations of eternity. To experience them we must be at liberty, free from the constraints imposed by law, morality, and religion. The scientific, moral, and material world with its repressive, constricting conditions, is just what stands in the way of our ability to approach the eternal. Blake's is a very different vision of heaven from the one which requires self-suppression to achieve. At the root of Blake's creed is the belief that when we are constrained and, consequently, must measure and count, we are kept from our encounters with the eternal. We are kept away from ourselves, locked inside social, economic, and religious systems which enslave us. We are cut off from what Blake called energy. "I must create a system or be enslaved by another man's," Blake wrote in *The Four Zoas*. Concretely, Blake expressed this attitude when he wrote to John Trussler, who had commissioned several engravings from him and then faulted his execution because Blake had not wrought them according to his exact specifications:

I attempted every morning for a fortnight together to follow your Dictate, but when I found my attempts were in vain,

resolvd to shew an independence which I know will please an
Author better than slavishly following the track of another,
however admirable that track may be. (King 132)

In the energy, in the enthusiasm and innocent encounter with
experience that he found in children—in their capacity for sweet
delight—Blake saw a connection with life that was deeper than a
mathematical understanding of nature or a dutiful compliance with law.
The idea of childhood contact with the eternal was the model for his
entire vision of what true human being is before it is warped by science
and industry, when it still has the faculty of spontaneous perception
rather than molded perception and when our actions are our own rather
than the motions imposed upon us by culture and commerce. In the
oppression of children and in the subversion of their energy and delight
he saw the model of the oppression and perversion of mankind. In the
education of children he saw a system designed to stifle the sense of life.
This is from "The School Boy," in *The Songs of Experience*:

> … to go to school in a summer morn
> O! it drives all joy away;
> Under a cruel eye outworn,
> The little ones spend the day,
> In sighing and dismay.
>
> Ah then at times I drooping sit,
> And spend many an anxious hour.
> Nor in my book can I take delight,
> Nor sit in learnings bower,
> Worn thro' with the dreary shower
>
> How can the bird that is born for joy,
> Sit in a cage and sing.
> How can a child when fears annoy,
> But droop his tender wing,
> And forget his youthful spring,
>
> O! father & mother, if buds are nip'd,
> And blossoms blown away,

And if the tender plants are strip'd
Of their joy in the springing day,
By sorrow and cares dismay,

How shall the summer arise in joy
Or the summer fruits appear
Or how shall we gather what griefs destroy
Or bless the mellowing year,
When the blasts of winter appear.

In the operation of the authoritarian system which devitalized childhood
he saw the root of:

A murderous Providence! A creation that groans, living on Death,
Where Fish & Bird & Beast & Man & Tree & Metal & Stone
Live by Devouring. (Bronowski 119)

The nature of the spirit world that Blake perceived and represented in
his art and poetry is not fixed. It is contingent upon the nature of our
material existence.

VISION AND ART

Blake expressed his criticism of the temporal world and
documented his approach to eternity by translating his visions into art,
particularly by engraving and painting them onto copper plates in
images and words. In that hard medium he attempted to represent
something eternal and spiritual which transcended the accidents—the
matter—it used for representing itself, whether in art or nature. Because
Blake sees the spirit of something as more real than the matter through
which it reveals itself and because he conceives spirit to be the energy of
creation and perception, Blake anticipates the Phenomenology of
twentieth century philosophers like Edmund Husserl, who asserts that
perception is a function of the nature and character of the perceiver
more than of the thing perceived.

I see Every thing I paint In This World, but Every body does
not see alike. To the Eyes of a Miser a Guinea is more

beautiful than the Sun, & a bag worn with the use of Money
has more beautiful proportion than a Vine filled with
Grapes.... [T]o the Eyes of a Man of Imagination, Nature is
Imagination itself ...To Me This World is all One continued
Vision of Fancy or Imagination. (Ackroyd 209)

Blake's visionary faculty, encouraged, perhaps, by the moody
historical and spiritual resonance of Westminster Abbey had been with
him from his childhood. His first vision occurred, he told his wife, when
he was four. He saw God, who "put his head to the window and set
[Blake] screaming." (Ackroyd 34) In his *Life of Blake*, a mid-nineteenth-
century biography, Alexander Gilchrist reports that

> [o]n Peckham Rye (by Dulwich Hill) it is, as he will in
> after years relate, that while quite a child, of eight or ten
> perhaps, he has his "first vision". Sauntering along, the boy
> looks up and sees a tree filled with angels, bright angelic
> wings bespangling every bough like stars.... Another time,
> one summer morn, he sees the haymakers at work, and amid
> them angelic figures walking. (Ackroyd 34)

When Blake as a child told his mother "that he saw the Prophet Ezekiel
under a Tree in the Fields," she hit him for lying, and later, when he told
his parents of the vision of the tree full of angels, Alexander Gilchrist
reported "only through his mother's intercession" did he escape "a
thrashing from his honest father, for telling a lie." (Ackroyd 34)

Explain or explain away Blake's visions however one may, Blake
nevertheless actually experienced them, really and literally saw them as
sense perception. Along with this ability he also possessed the faculty for
representing what he saw. The very vision of Ezekiel that came to the
child stayed with him until it was sketched in pen in the early 1780s by
the man—as the prophet Ezekiel, not under a tree, but praying,
kneeling, and eyes cast up to heaven, by the bedside of a dying wife.

Blake began to draw around the age of three. His speech, from
childhood, was forthright and imaginative. In response to a visitor's
report of the grandeur of a foreign city, the child Blake said, "Do you
call *that* splendid? I should call a city splendid in which the houses
were of gold, the pavements of silver, the gates ornamented with

precious stones." (Ackroyd 34–5) Not only did Blake see visions but he actually conversed with the persons in the visions, whether God, Jesus, or his dead brother Robert. In a vision Robert elucidated the new method of engraving that allowed Blake to combine words and images on the same copper plate. In another vision—after he had read a passage in Edward Young's *Night Thoughts*, which Blake had been commissioned to illustrate, in which Young exclaimed, "Who can paint an angel?'—Blake was visited by the angel Gabriel. "Who can paint an angel?" Blake repeated to himself. Then he saw "a greater light than usual," and heard a voice say "Michael Angelo could."

> And how do *you* know? [Blake asked.]
> I *know* because I sat to him: I am the arch-angel Gabriel.
> Oho! You are, are you? [Blake challenged} I must have better assurance than that of a wandering voice; you may be an evil spirit—there are such in this land.
> You shall have good assurance, [the voice replied]. Can an evil spirit do this?
> [Blake] looked whence the voice came, and was then aware of a shinning shape with bright wings, who diffused much light. 'As I looked, the shape dilated more and more; he waved his hands; the roof of my study opened; he ascended into heaven; he stood in the sun, and beckoning to me, moved the universe.' (Ackroyd 195)

TEMPER AND INTENSITY

Although the anecdote of his sketching the exposed and moldering corpse of Edward I provides a fitting introduction to Blake as a visionary artist engaged with the eternal, it, nevertheless, does not give a full account of his character. Another incident from the time of his apprenticeship limning sepulchral figures on scaffolding in Westminster Abbey can serve to.

Attached to Westminster Abbey was a school whose boys used the Abbey—strange as it might appear now—as a playground and skittle alley i.e., a bowling alley. Thus, sometimes, while Blake hovered on scaffolding over one tomb or another, the boys ran around Westminster

Abbey playing. Part of their play often consisted in trying to annoy Blake in his work. One of the boys

> after having already tormented him … got upon some pinnacle on a level with his Scaffold in order better to annoy him. In the impetuosity of his anger, worn out with Interruption, [Blake] knocked him off & precipitated him to the ground, upon which he fell with terrific Violence. (Ackroyd 55)

Several other accounts reveal Blake as a man of temper and as a man whose temper was ignited by acts of injustice. They bear mentioning particularly because they involve issues central to themes in Blake's work. One of them directly concerns the treatment of children:

> Blake was standing at one of his Windows … & saw a Boy hobbling along with a log to his foot such an one as is put on a Horse or Ass to prevent their straying … Blakes blood boiled & his indignation surpassed his forebearance, he sallied forth, & demanded in no very quiescent terms that Boy should be loosed & that no Englishman should be subjected to those miseries, which he thought were inexcusable even towards a Slave. (Ackroyd 155)

When the boy's father showed up at Blake's door to demand upon what grounds Blake might challenge his parental authority, the two nearly came to blows until their argument ended in "mutual forgiveness & mutual respect." (King 70)

Another instance of Blake's active indignation at injustice concerns a woman being beaten in the street. "Seeing once, somewhere about St Giles's, a wife knocked about by some husband or other violent person, in the open street," Blake attacked him "with such counter violence of reckless and raging rebuke … that he recoiled and collapsed." (Ackroyd 155)

THE EIGHTEENTH CENTURY

Visionary and irascible, Blake was very much a man of the eighteenth-century. He strongly reacted against many of its hallmarks and he profoundly responded to it in and by his art, perhaps most tellingly by his focus on contraries. The eighteenth century was a century of contraries. Science, philosophy, politics, religion, manufacture were all undergoing attack, redefinition, and development. Rationalism rather than monarchy was becoming authoritative, and rebellion in the name of rationalism liberated the human spirit, but in the French Revolution, the rebellion founded on reason and "the rights of Man" soon became irrational, giving way to the chaotic and brutal explosion of the human spirit in the Reign of Terror in 1793.

This terrible manifestation of rebellion caused a retreat from the earlier radicalism with which many of the hopeful young of that era had been infused. William Wordsworth, a firebrand of the 1790s, became a foremost establishmentarian of the nineteenth century. Politically and temperamentally, Blake was among the party of the rebellious against authority, whether social or intellectual, whenever it enslaved or stymied visionary and imaginative capability, and he never abandoned his radicalism. Blake understood the Reign of Terror as an eruption of energy, inevitable because that energy had been suppressed. He did not revert to rationalism, either, like the deistic radicals he knew, but kept his faith in energy, vision, and the spirit. His late epics treat of the conflicts in their realm.

Blake's way of working and distributing his work was subversive, too. It owed more to the cottage culture of the early eighteenth century than to the factory culture incipient at the century's end. The sort of medieval craftsmanship that William Morris self-consciously attempted towards the end of the nineteenth century, Blake practiced with a conservative dedication that was radical during the first decades of the century. His studio was in his home, which was usually small, and every task was done by his hand or his wife Catherine's. The production of his books was itself as much a part of his art as the books themselves. The spirit was as engaged in their manufacture as it was in drawing or composing verse. And part of the matter of his work concerned the way the factory system and machinery injured the spirit and maimed the body:

> Wheel without wheel,
> To perplex youth in their outgoings & to bind to labours in
> Albion

Of day & night the myriads of eternity: that they may grind
And polish brass & iron hour after hour, laborious task,
Kept ignorant of its use: that they might spend the days of wisdom
In sorrowful drudgery to obtain a scanty pittance of bread.

(Bronowski 91)

The focus on the phenomenon of contraries as a dominant eighteenth century force is most familiarly presented in Dickens' famous first sentences of *A Tale of Two Cities*. But the interplay of contraries is at the heart of Blake's thought and his art. In this he anticipated the Hegelian and Marxist dialectics by several decades. Blake's work systematically sets aspects, whether of the century or of human conditions or characteristics against one another—innocence and experience, for example. Or he offers the vibrant energy of an eternal substance, the human spirit, in place of the fixity of the calibrating eye and the rational mind, which are bound by the world of matter and mechanism.

In part, just because the eighteenth century was an age of enlightenment, reason, and classical precision, it also was an age of visionary rebellion, passion, and romantic excess. Each calls the other into being. It was a time of pivotal historical change, when the character of the modern world was formed. Consequently, it was a time of fundamental religious, social, political, and cultural clashes. Significantly, too, the second half of the eighteenth century was the time of the two great, enduring, and definitive revolutions, the American colonial revolution against England and the French national revolution of an oppressed class against the aristocracy. The American Revolution was a rational revision and reapplication of accepted forms of governance and class distinction. It challenged autocratic and tyrannical power, but accepted class structure. It was one of the formative events of Blake's youth. The French Revolution was a visionary explosion of the human spirit. It challenged the very nature and definition of human relationships and the idea of class structured society. It was the formative event of his manhood. Both revolutions, although in different ways, set the ideas of authority and liberty against each other and established the tension that arose from their antagonism as the definitive philosophical and political issue for the centuries to follow, even up to the present day.

The spirit of liberty tearing off mind forged manacles provided the energy of rebellion. Laws, rules, and obligations hobbled the spirit for the sake of providing material wealth for a dominant class. The life of London fed the grim "Satanic Mills." People crippled by the engines of constraint developed compensatory visions and sensations which do violence to the human spirit. They have wrong visions. They "make up" Blake wrote in the version of "THE Chimney Sweeper" in *The Songs of Experience*, "a heaven of our misery."

In Blake's thought spiritual vitality depends upon social circumstances, and in his art he developed a critique of religious, moral, and political systems which thwart vitality. His work asserted a vision of a social and spiritual system congruent with eternal nature. The conditions of life must enable the complex of energy, perception, creation, and pleasure:

> "Five windows light the cavern'd Man: thro' one he breathes
>   the air;
> "Thro' one hears music of the spheres; thro' one the eternal
>   vine
> "Flourishes, that he may recieve the grapes; thro' one can
>   look
> "And see small portions of the eternal world that ever
>   groweth;
> "Thro' one himself pass out what time he please. (Lister 62)

Blake believed that the rules of the state, the church, and the schools along with the restraints imposed by commercialism and the needs of mechanized factory production waste, punish and destroy human energy and are at the root of human evil and misery. The following is part of the version of "A Little BOY Lost" that appears in *The Songs of Experience*:

> ... Father...................
> I love you like the little bird
> That picks up crumbs around the door
> The Priest sat by and heard the child.
> In trembling zeal he seiz'd his hair:
> He led him by his little coat:
> And all admir'd the Priestly care.

....

They stripp'd him to his little shirt,
And bound him in an iron chain.

And burn'd him in a holy place,
Where many had been burn'd before.

Crippling the sexual capacity, closing the one of the "five windows ...
[t]hro' [which] one himself pass[es] out what time he please," by
"burn[ing the child] in a holy place" is for Blake one of the principle evils
of conventional social, religious and industrial practices and one of the
fundamental means of denying our eternal nature and our capacity for
sweet delight.

In the eighteenth century the conflict between liberty and authority
found expression in the opposing classical and gothic styles. The classical
represented respect for the prevailing order and a proper suppression of
self, the gothic, rebellion against prevailing systems and liberation of
self. An obvious example of the classical mode can be seen in the poetry
of Alexander Pope with its well wrought couplets, its witty homiletic
wisdom and its satire of human aspiration and human foible. Gothic,
which is most notably expressed in the architecture of churches, became
an influential literary force, too, during the second half of the eighteenth
century. It is the mode of such works as the literary forgery *The
Wanderings of Ossian* by James Macpherson or Horace Walpole's rather
bizarre and hysterical *The Castle of Otranto.* In works like these, ruling
social values are caricatured and attacked, and the class of individuals
who uphold those systems is portrayed as predatory while those who
suffer their power are portrayed as prey.

Formally, the contrast between classic and gothic styles is a contrast
between art organized around a set of impersonal rules and produced
inside a culture with which the artist is comfortable, even if critical—the
classic, and art which is organized around the particularities of a quirky,
perhaps even disturbed sensibility, a sensibility which is alienated from
and uncomfortable inside its culture, or at least, strives to be
independent of its culture—the gothic. The gothic dictates its form
rather than conform, as classical work does, to rules. Gothic is a spirit as
well as a form, John Ruskin explained some twenty years after Blake's
death in "The Nature of Gothic" in *The Stones of Venice.* Considering

gothic architecture, Ruskin wrote "the characteristic or moral elements of Gothic are the following ... 1. Savageness. 2. Changefulness. 3. Naturalism. 4. Grotesqueness. 5. Rigidity. 6. Redundance." Ruskin goes on to explain that "[t[hese characters are here expressed as belonging to the building; as belonging to the builder they would be expressed thus:— 1. Savageness or Rudeness. 2. Love of Change. 3. Love of Nature. 4. Disturbed imagination. 5. Obstinacy. 6. Generosity." Ruskin not only defines and anatomizes the gothic but he leaves the suggestion—when he defines the characteristics of the gothic from the point of view of the created work and of the work's creator—that there are visible emanations from an invisible world, one of Blake's bedrock beliefs. The building represents the vision, the attitude, the spirit of the builder. (Ruskin 171) Ruskin's essay, like Blake's way of working and his social critique, insists on the value of the individual as an individual who must retain the power to determine what he will do in his work. The worker must be seen as a visionary artisan rather than as an automaton engaged in mechanized production. For Blake as it would be for Ruskin, the fundamental issue is the contrast between individual craftsmanship, even when carried out by the collective, cooperative effort of a group of independent artisans, and the mindless toil of industrial workers who become nothing more than parts of the machinery in a factory. "Execution," Blake held, "is only the result of invention." When "Manual Labor" is treated like the operation of a machine, workers are merely "Ignorant Journeymen" and their work is the "work of no Mind." When work becomes imitation not invention, not the creation of an outline, but merely filling it in—whether in the fine arts or in the making of goods—"that which is Soul & Life" is "turn[ed] into a Mill or Machine." Machinery Blake maintained is "Destructive of Humanity & of art."(Ackroyd 293ff.)

Not only does Blake's work have a gothic quality, but Blake, in his spirit and attitude towards his work and towards his society is a gothic artist. Formally he was guided by the requirements of his imagination rather than by the rules of aesthetics. That Blake's art was gothic, however, does not mean it is primitive or lacks intellect. Blake was a conscious and a self-conscious artist: "I know my Execution is not like Any Body Else I do not intend it should be so:" (Erdman 571)

Men think they can Copy Nature as Correctly as I copy
Imagination this they will find Impossible. & all the Copies
or Pretended Copiers of Nature from Rembrandt to
Reynolds Prove that Nature becomes to its Victim nothing
but Blots & Blurs. Why are Copiers of Nature Incorrect
while Copiers of Imagination are Correct this is manifest to
all." (Erdman 563)

BLAKE'S FIRST BIOGRAPHERS

Any biography of William Blake is seriously indebted to the *Life of
William Blake*, published in 1863 and attributed to Alexander Gilchrist,
but actually written by Gilchrist and his wife, Anne, who worked on the
book with him and completed it after his early death at thirty-three. It
was not the first biography of William Blake. That was by Frederick
Tatham, who knew Blake and his wife during Blake's last years and who
took Blake's wife in as housekeeper after Blake's death. But the
Gilchrists' was the biography that brought fame to Blake. His *Songs of
Innocence and of Experience* engraved and hand-painted had sold fewer
than twenty copies during his lifetime. The Prophetic Books, *The Four
Zoas, Milton, Jerusalem, America*, and *The French Revolution* were virtually
unknown. Robert Southey, the Poet Laureate of England then,
dismissed Blake as "a man of great, but undoubtedly insane genius." In
1824, three years before Blake's death, when Charles Lamb sent one of
Blake's chimney sweeper poems to James Montgomery for inclusion in
his socially conscious *Chimney-Sweeper's Friend and Climbing Boy's Album*,
in hopes of getting laws passed to help such workers, Lamb was unaware
that Blake was still alive. (Bronowski 158) In 1830 a six volume
encyclopedia entitled *Lives of the Most Eminent British Painters* by Alan
Cunningham appeared. In it Blake was given a brief mention and
characterized as "a lovable, minor eccentric: unworldly, self-taught and
self-deluded." (Holmes, *http:// books. guardian.co.uk/ departments/
classics/story/0,6000,1227029,00.html*)
    Alexander Gilchrist actually spoke with people like Samuel Palmer,
who had been one of the young men who had formed a circle of
devotees—they called themselves The Ancients—around the aged
Blake, and with Henry Crabb Robinson who had recorded his
conversations with Blake. In 1811, Robinson had published an article in

a German magazine entitled "William Blake: Artist, Poet, and Religious Dreamer." When the Gilchrists' biography was published in 1863, it was received enthusiastically by such important mid-Victorians as Dante Gabriel Rossetti, Robert Browning, and A.C. Swinburne. It set in motion the publication of Blake's work—William Butler Yeats was his first editor—rescued him from obscurity, and began the process of establishing him as a great poet, painter, engraver, and visionary.

His Early Years

William Blake was born on November 28, 1757, the third of five children, in London. His father, James Blake was a hosier. He made and sold woven and knitted goods, stockings, socks, night-caps, and gloves. In 1752, he had married Catherine Hermitage, the daughter and the widow of hosiers, thereby getting a wife and expanding his business. His shop was on the street level and the family lived above the shop. The neighborhood was filled with small tradesmen—engravers, harpsichord-makers, carpenters. Respectably middle class, it was beginning, nevertheless, to decline. William was baptized on December 11th in the nearby great domed church of Saint Paul's, designed by Christopher Wren.

The Blakes were, however, in matters of religion, Dissenters, although there is no record indicating a specific sect to which they belonged. The fundamental principle of Dissent was opposition to the Creeds and the offices of the Church of England. Dissenters believed that

> Christ was the ... head of the Church and Scripture was the only rule of faith and practice. Faith [for Dissenters] was left to the individual to encounter in his own way and by the power of reason invested in his own private judgment.

Dissent, thus

> signifies the shift from a reliance upon external authority in moral matters, to the internal authority of the self informed by reason. This shift was in part traditional, and in part inspired by the seventeenth century Newtonian world outlook.... [A]n

appeal was made to experience and conscious knowledge of the world of material nature. While the mysteries of Christianity were to be located and expelled, there was a simultaneous effort to preserve the virtues of Christianity while adjusting them to the new rationalistic and scientific temper. (*www.historyguide.org/intellect/dissenter.html*)

There was, however, another branch of Dissent less beholden to rationalism. It has roots in Rational Dissent and in a belief in the primacy of individual spiritual experience unmediated by Church rules, but it is, at the same time, a pole apart from rationalism. Rational Dissent turns Christianity into a moral philosophy validated by reason. Rational Dissent values the reality and the laws of the material world. Christianity and science, accordingly, can be seen to be in harmony with each other. This is a view to which Blake strongly objected, as he indicated when he wrote that if Christianity were a moral philosophy Socrates would be as much God as Jesus. If the spiritual world can reveal itself to individuals without the mediation of the Church, as Dissenters believed, it may also reveal itself through visionary experience, as it did for Blake.

The Dissent of the visionaries as opposed to that of the rationalists was rooted in the philosophy of Emmanuel Swedenborg, a visionary prophet and mystic. His mystical influence often existed alongside the newly secular view of the world as matter subject to scientific law. James Blake's beliefs encompassed Rational Dissent and Swedenborg, and William read Swedenborg at a young age. Thus science and revelation coexisted in Blake's father's household. Additionally, Swedenborg's thought exercised a particular fascination on the young Blake's imagination because, for Swedenborg, 1757, the year of Blake's birth, was prophetically significant: "The Last Judgment was accomplished in the spiritual world in the year 1757 ... the former heaven and the former earth are passed away and all things are become New.' (Ackroyd 18)

Like most dissenters, Blake's father was a political radical, opposed to George III's war against the American colonists, liberal and egalitarian in his social policies. He practiced his social values in his private life, too. Seeing that his son William

despised restraints & rules, so much [he] dare not send him to School. Like the Arabian Horse, [William Blake] is said to have so hated a Blow that his Father thought it most prudent to withhold from him the liability of receiving punishment. He picked up his Education as well as he could.

"Thank God," Blake rhymed years later, "I never was sent to school/ To be Flogd into following the Style of a Fool. (Ackroyd 23) A vigorous and active boy, daring and impetuous, he was allowed to wander about freely "among the haymakers on the outskirts of London" and "about the quiet neighborhood streets." (Ackroyd 30, 32)

Although, Blake later wrote, "There is no use in education, I hold it wrong. It is the great Sin. It is eating of the tree of the knowledge of Good and Evil," (Ackroyd 23) it seems reasonable to assume he means schooling. When he wrote that "Man Brings All that he has or Can have Into This World with him. Man is Like a Garden ready Planted & Sown," (Ackroyd 23) Blake seems to mean that our capacities both to know and to create are not enhanced by learning but are already set in us. But in neither utterance it seems was he condemning study. Blake wrote in the marginalia to the writings of Sir Joshua Reynolds, a painter he detested, that "The Bible says That Cultivated Life Existed First—Uncultivated Life comes afterwards from Satans Hirelings." (Erdman 626) In a letter, moreover, he wrote that he was one who "has not lost any of his life since he was five years old without incessant labor & study." (Ackroyd 23) "I am happy I cannot say," Blake wrote in his marginalia to Joshua Reynolds' *Works*, "that Rafael Ever was from my Earliest Childhood hidden from Me. I saw & I Knew immediately the difference between Rafael & Rubens." (Erdman 627) He also wrote that he "read [political philosopher Edmund] Burkes Treatise when very Young at the same time I read [English philosopher, John] Locke on Human Understanding & [essayist, Sir Francis] Bacons Advancement of Learning ... I felt the Same Contempt & Abhorrence then; that I do now." (Ackroyd 25) Moreover, his juvenile attempts at verse show familiarity with Edmund Spenser and Ben Jonson. (Ackroyd 38) At the age of ten, he was reading the poetry of Thomas Chatterton in *Town and Country Magazine*. (Ackroyd 40) It is probable, too, that the child Blake read nursery rhymes, Aesop's fables and illustrated books for children. The most important book of his youth, one he read repeatedly and closely, was the Bible. It was central in the life of Dissenters and it is apparent throughout his work. In his later years he learned Hebrew, and in order to read Dante, he taught himself Italian.

Blake's parents not only respected their son's temperament with regard to schooling. They did not force his career direction, either. Unlike his father and his older brother, James, Blake was ill-fitted for shop keeping. Young William Blake was "totally destitute of the dexterity of a London shopman" and was "sent away from the counter as a booby." Blake's father did encourage his son's aptitude for and interest in writing and drawing, however. He bought prints of antique works like "the Gladiator, the Hercules, [and] the Venus of Medicis." The young Blake himself soon began frequenting print shops and collecting prints (which the poverty of his old age demanded he sell during his last years). (Ackroyd 36–8)

When he was ten, Blake's parents enrolled him in Henry Pars' Drawing School, a preparatory school for the Academy of Painting and Sculpture, which had been established by the great eighteenth-century engraver of satirical pictures of English dissipation, William Hogarth. Blake spent five years at Pars' and was trained in draughtsmanship and given engraved prints and plaster casts as models. He was also made to copy engravings by Durer, Adam Ghisi's engravings of works by Michelangelo, and sketches of temples, public buildings, and statues of the classical past from Greece and Asia Minor that Pars' brother, William, had gathered on an expedition through the region. In his second year, Blake was allowed "to draw from the casts of classical sculpture in the Duke of Richmond's Gallery in Whitehall" where he drew such classical statuary as the Apollo Belvedere and probably worked with notable teachers and painters of the time like Giovanni Cipriani, Joseph Wilton, and John Hamilton Mortimer. (Ackroyd 37)

After Pars' Drawing School, Blake might have sought a painter to tutor him and then applied to the Royal Academy Schools in order to study painting. Instead, he became an apprentice to the engraver James Basire:

> [I]t was deemed necessary to place him under some Tutor a painter of eminence [and] necessary applications were made[. Because of] the huge premium required, [Blake] requested with his characteristic generosity that his Father would not on any account spend so much money on him; as he thought

it would be an injustice to his brothers & sisters; he therefore himself proposed Engraving as being less expensive & sufficiently eligible for his future avocations. (Ackroyd 40)

Engraving was, in fact, becoming an exceptionally popular and profitable business in London. As an engraver's apprentice, Blake would learn a trade and also be able to continue his study of drawing. On August 4, 1772, therefore, Blake was apprenticed to James Basire for a period of seven years. His father paid a fee of fifty-two pounds, ten shillings. Henry Pars brother William had worked with Basire on sketches of his, and Pars probably recommended him.

As an engraver, Basire followed traditional methods—he had been held in high regard by Hogarth—eschewing newer techniques like mezzotint, whereby a roughened surface is scraped or polished so that an impression of light and shade is produced. Basire favored strong outlining and precise delineation of form. It was a severe and powerful style. Blake had seen examples of it in the engravings of such masters as Durer and Raphael. Although Basire was considered old-fashioned and said to have a "dry and monotonous manner" of engraving, it was precisely this aspect of the art that Blake wished to master, disliking the soft and painterly new techniques. (Ackroyd 43) For Blake, invention and creativity lay in outlining. Shading or filling in subordinated the craftsman to another artist's vision.

Basire was a good and kind master, and he and Blake got on well. Blake's work primarily involved doing illustrations of scientific instruments for volumes like the *Philosophical Transactions* of the Royal Society. He also illustrated treatises concerned with archeology and mythology. For *A New System, or, An Analysis of Ancient Mythology* by Jacob Bryant, Blake probably engraved a moon ark with a dove and a rainbow. (Ackroyd 45) At the age of sixteen, he engraved the first work which might be called Blakean and which Blake himself valued. It was the figure of *Joseph of Arimathea among The Rocks of Albion*. Blake kept the copper plate for the rest of his life and made proofs of it as late as 1825. It was during the period of his apprenticeship with Basire, too, that Blake made his sketches of the monuments and of the disinterred king at Westminster Abbey. At this time, too, Blake perfected the skill of writing backwards, mirror writing, which proved essential when he engraved words and images together on copper plates.

Blake continued his self-education, too. In 1773, he purchased *Historia del Testamento Vecchio (The Story of the Old Testament)* by Annibale Carracci, a collection of engravings. Blake's copy survives with his name and the date inscribed in it. From this volume, he copied details of several of the etchings included in it, and on the cover he drew a picture of the sun with a human face. (Ackroyd 59) He also studied painting on his own. He read Abbe Wincklemann's *Reflections on the Painting and Sculpture of the Ancient Greeks*. One of its principle tenets is the very Blakean idea that "the representation of invisible, past, and future things" is "the most eminent prerogative of painting." (Ackroyd 59) Blake always insisted that art's proper object of imitation is not nature or the actual material objects of the concrete world but the imagination.

At the same time that he was learning his craft as an engraver, Blake was studying the great English poets and reading histories of England which were as much mythological as historical. He read Milton's *History of Britain* as well as *Paradise Lost* and *Samson Agonistes*, and used it for subject matter for the historical watercolor paintings he executed during his apprenticeship. At around the age of twelve, too, he began writing verse, which was later published as *Poetical Sketches*, and which shows the influence of the great English poets on him. Blake also was fascinated and influenced by two strange bodies of poetry, actually written by mid-eighteenth-century poets, but put forward as ancient works newly discovered, James Macpherson's *Ossian* and "Thomas Rowley's" medieval poetry, really by Thomas Chatterton, who poisoned himself at the age of seventeen. Dark brooding works of conflict and romance in expressionistically archaic language, they explore and map the landscape of the imagination rather than record authentic perceptions of the natural world and its actual conditions.

AT THE ROYAL ACADEMY SCHOOLS

After his period of apprenticeship, rather than join the Stationers' Guild and become a professional engraver, Blake applied to the Royal Academy to begin a formal study of painting. Tuition was free and competition for admission—twenty-five applicants were accepted each year—was intense. Blake submitted a drawing and it is probable that the artist James Barry was his sponsor. In August 1779, Blake was admitted to the Royal Academy Schools. During the first three months, as a probationer, Blake was required to work in the Antique Gallery using plaster models "to produce a complete and technically accurate anatomical drawing of the human figure." (Ackroyd 63) He did, and on October 8th he was enrolled in the Academy for six years.

At the Academy Blake seems to have deplored more of his training than he assimilated. True, he developed his skill in drawing the human anatomy, especially because after working in the Antique gallery, he was moved—upon being accepted into the school—to the Life Gallery where he drew from live nudes. But Blake continued to favor copying from art and from his imagination rather than from nature. He asserted paradoxically that in Westminster Abbey "he ... imbibed the pure & spiritual character of the female expression & form," and that life drawing was "hateful" and that it "smelled of mortality" rather than shone with spirit. "[M]odern Man stripped from his load of clothing," Blake is reported to have said, "is like a dead corpse." (Ackroyd 65) Thus, although it is undeniable that Blake learned something at the Academy about drawing and painting that served him as an engraver and a painter, he found the curriculum and many on the faculty antipathetical to his sense of art and life.

First among the faculty was the president of the school, the noted painter Sir Joshua Reynolds. Blake contemned the man and his painting. Blake particularly disliked the medium of oil, in which Reynolds worked. Blake preferred fresco or tempera, techniques of painting with a water, glue, or egg base. These old techniques had been supplanted by oil, but Blake found oil painting too sensuous and too blurred, muddy, and indistinct—not conducive to the production of strong outline. (Ackroyd 67) Reynolds himself had offended Blake when he advised him to work with "less extravagance and more simplicity" (Ackroyd 67) Blake's general attitude toward the school and the faculty is well illustrated by the following notation he made some twenty years later when reviewing Reynolds *Works*:

I was once looking over the Prints from Rafael & Michael Angelo. in the Library of the Royal Academy[.] [George Michael] Moser [a teacher and librarian at the Academy] came to me & said You should not Study these old Hard Stiff & Dry Unfinishd Works of Art, Stay a little & I will shew you what you should Study. He then went & took down

[French historical painter, 1619-1690, Charles] Le Bruns &
[Flemish painter, 1577–1640, Peter Paul] Rubens's.... How I
did secretly Rage. I also spoke my Mind[.] I said to Moser,
These things that you call Finishd are not Even Begun how
can they then, be Finishd? The Man who does not know The
Beginning, never can know the End of Art. (Ackroyd 68)

Blake did admire one painter teaching at the Royal Academy.
James Barry's taste and manner were similar to Blake's. His monumental
and heroic paintings showed the energy of a passionate wildness absent
from neo-classical painting. Like Blake, he admired Raphael,
Michelangelo, and Milton. He also engraved his own work, using bold
outlines, eschewing the tendency of the age to make art pretty. (Ackroyd
68) He was ultimately dismissed from the academy for his differences
with the predominating tendencies there. The way Barry was treated
while at the Academy reinforced Blake's indignation at the politics of the
contemporary art world:

Who will Dare to Say that Polite Art [i.e., Fine Art] is
Encouraged, or Either Wished or Tolerated in a Nation
where The Society for the Encouragement of Art. Sufferd
Barry to Give them, his Labour for Nothing ... Barry told me
that while he Did that Work-he Lived on Bread & Apples.
(Ackroyd 69)

Probably the most beneficial aspect of attending the Royal
Academy for Blake was meeting several young men with interests and
talents similar to his who became friends, supporters, and, sometimes,
benefactors. In many instances, however, Blake's friendships ended in
animosity when it began to appear to him that friends were hostile or
jealous of his genius.

His Circle

Blake met Thomas Stothard in 1779 during his first year at the
Royal Academy. Like, Blake, Stothard had a passionate admiration for
Durer's etchings, was dedicated to painting national historical subjects,
and was illustrating Macpherson's poems of Ossian. Stothard introduced

Blake to John Flaxman, the son of a plaster-cast maker. Although his name is unfamiliar today—although his sculpture can be seen at Westminster Abbey and St. Paul's Cathedral, and a Wedgwood vase of his design is at the Metropolitan Museum of Art in New York City—during the late eighteenth century Flaxman was famous as a painter, sculptor, and designer throughout Europe. He shared Blake's enthusiasm for gothic art, the tombs of Westminster Abbey, and the poetry of Chatterton, which he illustrated. Through Flaxman Blake entered London society although "in consequence of his unbending deportment, or what his adherents are pleased to call his manly firmness of opinion, which certainly was not at all times considered pleasing by everyone, his visits were not so frequent." (Ackroyd 87).

Flaxman had been slight and sickly youth who spent his childhood behind the counter in his father's shop studying by himself. There he was "discovered" by the Reverend Anthony Stephen Mathew, who took an interest in his education. Mathew's wife was a "Blue-stocking." The term reflects the intellectual and social subordination of women common to the time, for it refers to the anomaly of a woman who reads books and engages in intellectual conversation about such matters as art, literature, philosophy, and history. The Mathews' home, which Flaxman decorated with imitation stained glass and faux antique furniture and statuary, served as a literary and artistic salon. Flaxman brought Blake into this circle. In *Nollekens and His Ttimes*, published in 1845, which includes a short account of Blake's life, J.T. Smith recalls Blake at Mrs. Mathew's gatherings:

> At that lady's most agreeable conversaziones I first met the late William Blake, the artist, to whom she and Mr Flaxman had been truly kind. There I have often heard him read and sing several of his poems. He was listened to by the company with profound silence, and allowed by most of the visitors to possess original and extraordinary merit. (Ackroyd 85)

Smith's recollection not only serves to locate Blake and confirm Flaxman's importance to him but also reveals that Blake actually sang his poetry. According to Smith, although Blake "was entirely unacquainted with the science of music, his ear was so good, and his tunes were sometimes most singularly beautiful, [they] were noted down by musical

professors." (Lister 15) These notations have not survived. A record of
Blake's sojourn in society which has, is a manuscript he probably wrote
around 1784 called "An Island in the Moon," a burlesque of the
Mathews' circle mixing prose and verse and containing a glimpse of the
intellectual concerns and foibles of the time as well as early draughts of
some verses from *The Songs of Innocence.*

Blake's circle of close friends also included George Cumberland,
an insurance clerk, amateur artist, collector of Italian prints, an
aesthetician who later wrote several books about art, and a patron of his
needy friends. William Sharp was a professional engraver when Blake
met him, and he was a religious enthusiast and a follower of
Swedenborg. Thomas Taylor was a neo-Platonist, mystic, scientist who
shared Blake's contempt for John Locke, the industrial revolution,
commercialism, and materialist science.

Besides sharing similar attitudes about art and aesthetics, this circle
of friends was joined together by a common adherence to the radical
political doctrine of liberty, a dangerous position during the last decades
of the eighteenth century. England was at war with the American
colonies and with France. The political climate was such that in 1780
when Blake and Stothard went on an expedition up the Medway River
to do some pencil drawings, they were arrested. They had stopped on
the shore and as they were sketching, "they were suddenly surprised by
the appearance of ... soldiers, who very unceremoniously made them
prisoners, under the suspicion that they were spies for the French
government." They were put under armed guard and kept in a tent made
out of the sails from their boat until members of the Royal Academy
could be contacted who could verify their identities and their enrollment
in the school. (Ackroyd 73)

In 1780, too, unlike the mistake on the Medway, Blake was
involved in an event that did have an incendiary political agenda, the
Lord Gordon Riots in London. At the time that the parliament was
determining that restrictions against liberties of Catholics ought to be
rescinded, there was a violent street demonstration by Protestants
against "popery." Blake, apparently, was out walking and was swept up by
the crowd and carried along to the Old Bailey and Newgate Prison. The
prison was set on fire and the convicts released. Blake left the scene
unharmed and unrecognized. Those who were recognized subsequently
were hanged.

Around this time, Blake painted "Albion Rose," which he later engraved. It depicts a young man with arms flung wide apart in a gesture of freedom. There is a look of exultation on his face. Blake also made a series of paintings, "Fire," "Pestilence," and "A Breach in the City" which suggest times of social upheaval and the accompanying emotional drama. In addition, he did a number of biblical and historical watercolor paintings, like "The Death of Earl Goodwin," which were exhibited in the Royal Academy's ante-room—not in the main room where only oils were hung. Blake's exhibition was reviewed in the *Morning Chronicle and London Advertiser*. The writer, Blake's friend George Cumberland, praised Blake's work for "good design and much character." (Ackroyd 76)

Blake did his first commercial work in 1780, too: an engraving of a design by his friend Stothard. Over the next few years, Blake did a number of engravings for the *Novelist's Magazine*, *The Wit's Magazine*, a *Collection of English Songs*, *An Introduction to Mensuration* [measurement], and *An Introduction to Natural Philosophy*. He also provided a number of engravings for several editions of the Bible. It was routine work and relegated Blake to a subsidiary position, engraving works by other artists and to predetermined specifications. It was work he would continue to do throughout his life, producing nearly six hundred plates at the dawn of the era of mass production.

His Marriage

On August 18, 1782, Blake married Catherine Boucher, one of many children of a poor market gardener. Blake had met her in Battersea earlier that year when he went to visit relatives of his father and to recover from an unsuccessful courtship with a woman he had been seeing who had rejected his offer of marriage, and who had answered his objection to her seeing other young men with the sassy challenge, "Are you a fool?" Her sharp response, Blake later said, "cured me of jealousy." (Ackroyd 80) Blake met Catherine, according to her account, when he visited her parents at Battersea and told the story of his unhappy courtship. She voiced sympathy for him. "Do you pity me?" he asked her. "Yes indeed I do," she answered. "Then I love you," Blake said. For Catherine, it was love immediately. She reported that she "instantly recognized her future partner" when she first saw Blake enter the room and that she "was so near fainting that she left his presence until she had recovered." (Ackroyd 80)

For Blake it seems his love grew from her willingness, indeed, desire to pity him, i.e., to care for him and to take care of him. Their union lasted forty-five years until Blake's death, and it was a loving one. Despite Blake's dedication to liberty, it was founded on his predominance and her subservience. Blake's view was that "the female ... lives from the light of the male," (Ackroyd 83) a biblical precept John Milton reiterated in *Paradise Lost* when he wrote of Adam and Eve that he was created to serve God alone and she to serve God in him. It was not an arrangement with which Catherine Blake disagreed. She habitually sat beside him while he worked in order "to calm the turbulence of his thoughts." (Ackroyd 81) Although, she said, she did not always understand Blake's poems, "she was sure they had a meaning and a fine one." (Ackroyd 83) She learned to use a printing press, to color his proofs, and to hold his opinions herself as fervently as he did. She made his clothes and sang to him. As he lay dying, Blake drew her portrait and told her, "You have ever been an angel to me." She saw him in visions after his death and conversed with him. (Ackroyd 83)

There is one incident, however, which reflects ill on the quality of Blake's love for his wife and reveals both the stern tenor of his temperament and the nature of the division of the sexes which was common in the eighteenth century. The only person to be favored by Blake's love beside Catherine, and perhaps more highly than Catherine, was his youngest brother Robert, born in 1767, ten years after Blake, to whom Blake was devoted. He was Blake's companion and pupil. Blake taught him draughtsmanship, drew figures for Robert to copy, and Robert and William drew sketches of each other. Two of Robert's notebooks are extant. One is a sketchbook with anatomical drawings, drawings of dogs, drawings of ancient religious rites and of figures in threatening or supplicating postures. The other notebook served as a portfolio. Blake kept it with him all his life after Robert's death and used the blank pages in it for notes of his own, and in it are draughts of the *Songs of Experience.* (Ackroyd 84) Blake engraved one of Robert's drawings from this notebook, "The Approach of Doom."

Robert often visited Blake and Catherine at their home on Green Street in Leicester Square. On one visit, Robert and Catherine apparently had a disagreement about something—we don't know what—

and Catherine said something—again, we don't know what—to Robert which angered Blake. According to Catherine's later report, Blake commanded her to "[k]neel down and beg Robert's pardon directly or you never see my face again!" Although Catherine thought it "very hard" to comply, particularly because she thought she was not at fault in the argument, she did as Blake ordered, begged Robert's pardon and said, "I am in the wrong," whereupon Robert responded, "Young woman, you lie! *I* am in the wrong." In 1787, at the age of nineteen Robert died. Blake remained continuously at his bedside during the last two weeks of his life. After Robert's death, Blake slept for three days. Afterwards, he regularly communicated with him in dreams and visions:

> [W]ith his spirit I converse daily & hourly in the Spirit & See him in my remembrance in the regions of my Imagination. I hear his advice & even now write from his Dictate. (Ackroyd 100ff.)

HIS CAREER BEGINS

In 1882 Blake's first book of poetry, *Poetical Sketches*, was published. The Mathews and Flaxman paid for its printing, (Lister 15) which was done by Blake's old master Basire, and it was sold in Flaxman's aunt's print shop on the Strand. There is a Preface written by Blake's sponsors:

> The following Sketches were the production of untutored youth, commenced in his twelfth, and occasionally resumed by the author till his twentieth year; since which time, his talents having been wholly directed to the attainment of excellence in his profession, he has been deprived of the leisure requisite to such a revisal of these sheets, as might have rendered them less unfit to meet the public eye.
>
> Conscious of the irregularities and defects to be found in almost every page, his friends have still believed that they possessed a poetical originality, which merited some respite from oblivion. These their opinions remain, however, to be now reproved or confirmed by a less partial public. (Lister 15)

The combination of esteem and condescension suggested here helps to explain Blake's frequent fallings out with apparently well-meaning friends and relieves him of the imputations of unsteadiness which clung to him. He wrote retrospectively of Flaxman's preface and of a note Flaxman sent to the poet William Hayley along with a copy of *Poetical Sketches* hoping that Blake's "education will plead sufficient excuse to your liberal mind for the defects of his work" that Flaxman "blast[ed his] character as an artist." (Ackroyd 98) Such a disclaimer as that appended to his first poems could make any artist bristle. But it occurred at a time particularly galling, for during the early 1780s Blake was trying to establish his reputation as an artist. Besides publishing *Poetical Sketches*, in 1784 and 1785, he exhibited several of his watercolors, engravings, and drawings in the Exhibition Room of Sculpture and Drawings at the Royal Academy. To add to Blake's distress, the subscription his friends were attempting to collect for a trip to Rome so that Blake could study the great works of art there fell through. Flaxman, on the other hand, with the financial help of Josiah Wedgwood, the potter, traveled to Rome at this time, stayed there for seven years and returned to England with an international reputation. (Ackroyd 97)

Blake went into business. He opened a print shop with James Parker. The year was 1784. It was a potentially lucrative business at the time; the number of shops selling prints increasing dramatically during the last decades of the eighteenth century. Blake's father had just died after a long illness, and James Blake's eldest son, also called James, took over the hosiery shop and ran it, quite profitably, with his mother. William Blake and Catherine moved next door to the family's shop and dwelling, and his brother John opened a bakery across the street. Although Blake and Parker were both engravers, the principle business of their shop was selling prints, not making them. Nevertheless, the press that Blake bought at the time proved to be a good investment, for it enabled Blake to print his own work for the rest of his life, whether or not he could sell it. (Ackroyd 98)

Whether his brother Robert's death was the cause of Blake's interest in Swedenborg's theology or coincidental to it is impossible to determine without documentary evidence, of which there is none. But there is evidence that Blake began an intensive study of Swedenborg in 1787. And the connection between Robert's death and Blake's absorption in Swedenborg seems likely because Swedenborg's belief that "immediately on the death of the material body, (which will never be re-assumed), man rises again as to his spiritual or substantial body, wherein he existeth in perfect human form," exactly conforms to Blake's experience upon his brother's death as Gilchrist narrates it: "At the last solemn moment, [Blake] beheld the released spirit ascend heavenward through the matter-of-fact ceiling "clapping his hands for joy.'" (Ackroyd 102–3) Blake's heavily annotated copy of Swedenborg's *Arcane Coelestia, or Heaven and Hell* has survived. And in 1789, he and Catherine participated in a five-day conference of the New Jerusalem Church at the Swedenborgian Chapel in Great East Cheap.

Swedenborg was important to Blake not only because he described phenomenon Blake had experienced but because he valued the same apparatus for knowing as Blake, vision, not mechanistic science or repressive morality. He was a man, like Blake, who had "spoken with many spirits ... live[d] for years in company with spirits ... [and had] often been permitted to see the atmosphere of falsehood which exhales from hell." (Ackroyd 102) Like Blake, too, he brought the landscapes of heaven and hell into the sphere of the human landscape through the power of the visionary imagination and through a belief in the godly capacity of mortals:

> God is very Man. In all the heavens there is no other idea of God than that of a Man; the Reason is, because Heaven in the Whole, and in Part, is in Form as Man. By Reason that God is a Man, All Angels and Spirits are Men in a perfect Form. (Ackroyd 105)

Blake, characteristically, soon drew away from any kind of strict adherence to Swedenborgianism. He wanted no system but his own; nevertheless, the beliefs and terms of that system influenced and suffuse his work, particularly *The Marriage of Heaven and Hell*.

The late 1780s began a period of intense and extensive productivity. Blake was spurred on by his brother's death, by his fascination with Swedenborg, and by a set of engravings he was making for an English translation of the Swiss philosophical writer Johann Caspar Lavater's *Aphorisms on Man*. The translation was by Henry Fuseli, born in Switzerland, but living in England. Fuseli had been introduced to Blake by Flaxman: "When Flaxman was taken to Italy,"

Blake wrote, "Fuseli was given to me for a season." (Ackroyd 104) Fuseli was similar to Blake in his likes and dislikes—he admired Milton and Shakespeare, Michelangelo and Raphael, form and line in painting over color and shading, and like Blake, he preferred to draw from vision rather than from life. (Ackroyd 105) He often remarked that Blake was an influence upon him and that he borrowed from Blake and executed Blake's designs in his own work.

As with Swedenborg's *Heaven and Hell*, Blake's copy of Lavater's *Aphorisms* survives with his marginalia, annotations which Gilchrist called "god-dust," because they seem to show Blake's thought forming and in many cases are precursory formulations—"All life is holy," "Active evil is better than Passive Good"—of ideas which soon after, in 1790, appeared in *The Marriage of Heaven and Hell*. (Ackroyd 107)

In the years after Blake's brother Robert's death, from 1788 through 1796 Blake produced *All Religions Are One*, *There Is No Natural Religion*, the first of his illuminated works, *Songs of Innocence*, *The Book of Thel*, *Tiriel*, *The Marriage of Heaven and Hell*, *The French Revolution*, *America: A Prophecy*, *Visions of the Daughters of Albion*, *For Children: The Gates of Paradise*, *Songs of Innocence and of Experience*, *The First Book of Urizen*, *The Song of Los*, *The Book of Ahania*, *The Book of Los*, and he began writing *Vala, or The Four Zoas*. In addition, Blake produced twelve large color-printed drawings, illustrated Mary Wollstonecraft's *Original Stories from Real Life*, engraved *Albion Rose*, and made over five hundred water color illustrations for Edward Young's *Night Thoughts* for the publisher Richard Edwards, of which he finally engraved only forty. Blake had asked a hundred guineas for the job, but accepted twenty, although there were engravers like William Sharp who earned twelve hundred guineas for a single work. (Ackroyd 197)

During this period of intense creativity, Blake was hardly recognized for his own genius. When he worked with Fuseli—who enjoyed considerable recognition, became Professor of Painting at the Royal Academy, and regularly contributed articles to Joseph Johnson' *Analytical Review*—he was the subordinate partner just as he was when he did engraving for the Wollstonecraft or Young books. Blake was also ignored when John and Josiah Boydell established what became known as the "Shakespeare Gallery"; the famous artists of the day [were] invited to paint scenes from Shakespeare's works, which in 1789 were hung in an especially built gallery at No. 52 Pall Mall, while the best engravers [were commissioned to] produce a portfolio of prints from these works that could be purchased by subscription. The great artists and engravers of the day were asked ... with the single most obvious exception of William Blake.

To be excluded like this while friends and acquaintances prospered embittered Blake, but some years later, Blake wrote "I thank God that I courageously pursued my course through darkness." (Ackroyd 108)

It was at this time—Blake was working on *Tiriel*—that he had the vision in which his dead brother Robert revealed the process of relief etching to him. Rather than being engraved into the copper blocks, the matter to be printed was raised up from the copper block through the application of corrosives to the parts of the plate that were not to be printed. This method allowed the copper plates to be inked and printed or painted so that color images could be struck. It also allowed Blake to be his own printer and not rely on others to publish his work.

BETWEEN ART AND COMMERCE

Although he was largely denied recognition for his genius, Blake was recognized for his craftsmanship during the last decade of the eighteenth century, and he and Catherine lived comfortably and prospered. They even were robbed of "Plate ... & clothes," valued at one hundred pounds. It is not clear whether the plate was silver household plate or copper plates for engraving. For a while they had a servant, too, but found it went against their temperament. Catherine Blake was strong and healthy and could not see having a servant do work she herself could do, and having a servant in the house made them uncomfortable. Blake had severed his partnership with James Parker, who remained at their shop in Soho, and moved from Poland Street, where he had lived around the corner from the shop to Lambeth, where he could rent a larger but cheaper house of nine or ten rooms. Lambeth had been marsh, but in 1790 was solid, and there were two bridges joining it to central London. (Ackroyd 133)

Much of the commercial work Blake did during the nineties was for a friend, the publisher Joseph Johnson. Blake did etchings of urinary tract stones for a surgery manual, engravings for the *Conjuror's Magazine*, engravings of Fuseli's paintings to illustrate Erasmus Darwin's *The Botanic Garden*, sketches of scenes from *Paradise Lost*, and catalogue engravings of pottery for Josiah Wedgwood's pottery firm, including an engraving of a Wedgwood copy of a cobalt blue glass amphora with white opaque nude cameo figures standing, sitting, or hovering in a pastoral setting, dating back to the first century B.C., known as the Portland, or Barbieri Vase, which is presently in the British Museum.

For Johnson Blake also illustrated the children's book, *Elements of Morality for the Use of Children with an Introductory Address to Parents*. It is likely that Blake's lost boy poems in the *Songs of Innocence* and the *Songs of Experience* were influenced by it. Similarly, Blake's engravings of tortured blacks, among them "A Negro hung alive by the Ribs to a Gallows" for John Gabriel Steadman's memoir, *Narrative, of Five Year's Expedition, against the Revolted Negroes of Surinam* influenced Blake's "The Little Black Boy." Although Blake was forced to divide his efforts between his own work and commercial work, nevertheless he drew from his wage labor for his art, even if only to contradict convention. But he had an enormous amount of work to do, and he often missed the deadline for his commercial assignments, and he often neglected to answer letters. (Ackroyd 135, 6) Blake's tardiness is attributable to the way he worked as well as to the amount of work he had: "[M]y Abstract folly hurries me often away while I am at work, carrying me over Mountains & Valleys, which are not Real, in a Land of Abstraction where Spectres of the Dead wander." He fell into daydreams and yielded to the visitation of visionary spirits.

There are reports that during this time Blake also tutored students in his craft. Frederick Tatham's account affords a glimpse of Blake's personality:

About this time [Blake] taught Drawing & was engaged for that purpose by some families of high rank ... after his lessons he got into conversation with his pupils, & was found so entertaining & pleasant, possessing such novel thoughts & such eccentric notions, with such jocose hilarity and amiable demeanour, that he frequently found himself asked to stay to dinner, & spend the Evening in the same interesting & lively manner, in which he had consumed the morning. (Ackroyd 137)

Another report reveals again the class awareness and sense of independence that the Blakes' dislike of having a servant revealed. Blake, according to this unverifiable report

> was recommended & nearly obtained an Appointment to teach Drawing to the Royal Family. Blake stood aghast ... because he would have been drawn into a class of Society, superior to his previous pursuits & habits; he would have been expected to live in comparative respectability, not to say splendour, a mode of life, as he thought, derogatory to the simplicity of his designs & deportment.... His friends ridiculed & blamed him by turns but Blake found an Excuse by resigning all his other pupils. (Ackroyd 137)

RELIGION, POLITICS, AND POETRY

During the years spent at Lambeth, Blake moved away from Swedenborg and towards Paracelsus and Jacob Boehme. (Ackroyd 147) Paracelsus (1493–1541) and Boehme (1575–1624) were radical visionary mystics whose doctrines combined the teachings of the "wise heathens" with the teachings of Christianity, mixing alchemical and cabalistic knowledge with Christian revelation. "They ... repudiated the supremacy of logic and reason while concentrating on the visual signs and emblems of the divine presence within the world." Paracelsus had written that "imagination is like the sun. The sun has a light which is not tangible; but which, nevertheless, may set a house on fire." How powerful must that assertion have been to Blake, who testified: "I know of no other Christianity and no other Gospel than the liberty both of body & mind to exercise the Divine Arts of Imagination." (Ackroyd 148) Boehme's mystical system also offered strong support for Blake's theology:

> Our whole doctrine is nothing else but an instruction to show how man may create a kingdom of light within himself ... He in whom this spring of divine power flows, carries

within himself the divine image and the celestial
substantiality. In him is Jesus born from the Virgin, and he
will not die in eternity. (Ackroyd 149)

Blake's repudiation of Swedenborg reflects a metaphysical
difference and a fundamental political conflict. Blake's social radicalism
was compromised by the direction Swedenborg's adherents were
following, whereas the teachings of Paracelsus and Boehme supported
it. When Blake first joined with Swedenborgians, theirs was a church
composed of "occultists, mesmerists, and magicians," i.e. independent
visionaries unbound by rules and formulated doctrines. But by 1790,
when Blake abandoned it, the New Church was becoming "ritualized
and institutionalized—it began ordaining ministers, and ... prescribing
their robes of worship." Church leaders now supported "the
Constitution and Government of their country" rather than the
"principles of infidelity and democracy. Rather than focusing on the
active virtue of charity, church leaders emphasized the duty of avoiding
sinfulness." (Ackroyd 147). This sort of thinking was anathema to
Blake, who in *The Marriage of Heaven and Hell* (1790) wrote such
aphorisms as: "Those who restrain desire, do so because theirs is weak
enough to be restrained," "Prisons are built with stones of Law,
Brothels with bricks of Religion," "You never know what is enough
unless you know what is more than enough," "As the caterpillar chooses
the fairest leaves to lay her eggs on, so the priest lays his curse on the
fairest joys," "Sooner murder an infant in its cradle than nurse unacted
desires," and "Jesus was all virtue and acted from impulse not from
rules." Perhaps most significantly, Blake asserted that "all Bibles or
sacred codes have been the cause of the following Errors," that
"Energy[,] called Evil[,] is alone from the Body ... Reason[,] called
Good[,] is alone from the Soul." As a corrective, Blake subverts the
biblical categories of good and evil: "Energy is the only life," and that
"Energy is Eternal Delight."
    Boehme was important to Blake, moreover because he formulated
the very Blakean proposition expressed by Blake memorably in the
quatrain

I will not cease from Mental Fight,
Nor shall my Sword sleep in my hand:

Till we have built Jerusalem
In Englands green & pleasant Land

when he wrote that "Man must be at war with himself if he wishes to be a heavenly citizen ... fighting must be the watchword, not with tongue and sword, but with mind and spirit, and not to give over." (Ackroyd 150)

As much as Blake disdained the Christian category of Sin, he practiced the Christian virtue of Charity. Tatham relates that

> [a] young man passed [Blake's] House daily whose avocations seemed to lead him backward & forward to some place of study, carrying a Portfolio under his Arm. He looked interesting & eager, but sickly. After some time Blake sent Mrs Blake to call the young man in; he came & he told them, that he was studying the Arts. Blake from this took a high interest in him & gave him every instruction possible.

The boy was sick and soon perished.

> [H]is illness was long & his sufferings were great during which time Mrs Blake or Blake never omitted visiting him daily & administering medicine, money, or Wine & every other requisite until death relieved their adopted of all earthly care & pain. Every attention, every parental tenderness, was exhibited by the charitable pair. (Ackroyd 154, 5)

Tathum's wording, "every parental tenderness," suggests that the boy had gained the kind of affection William and Catherine Blake would have felt for their own child. For that brief time, perhaps he was. They had no other child, except, for Blake, his brother Robert, who was dead. Blake's love was, concretely, a particular regard for particular persons. As an ideal, Blake understood that love was the emotional medium which joined all people together. Blake held that neither love nor communality could be enforced by law, religion, or any coercive system. Such systems devitalized people and simultaneously corrupted the spirit.

Blake did not have to harbor belief in liberty as a solitary hope, for

the times were such when battles were being fought to make liberty
rather than authority the basis of human intercourse and organization.
The political radicals who supported the idea of liberty were rationalists
who believed, like Mary Wollstonecraft, author of the *Vindication of the
Rights of Woman* (1792) in "the law of reason" and in "Rational religion."
When Tom Paine, the American author of the great revolutionary tracts
The Rights of Man and *Common Sense* told Blake that "religion was a law
& a tye to all able minds," i.e., a means of constraining spirit and
intelligence, Blake responded that the religion of Jesus, was a perfect law
of liberty." (Ackroyd 159) But Blake was not narrow in his understanding
of systems and formulations other than his own, as his defense of Tom
Paine against an attack by Bishop R. Watson in Watson's *Apology for the
Bible* shows:

> The Perversions of Christ's words & acts are attack'd by
> Paine & also the perversions of the Bible. Paine has not
> attacked Christianity. Watson has defended Antichrist. It
> appears to me Now that Tom Paine is a better Christian than
> the Bishop. (Bronowski 81)

Although Blake was not alone in his radical political adherence to
liberty, nevertheless, the danger of holding and broadcasting such
opinions was not weakened by strength in numbers. Blake's poem, *The
French Revolution*, set in type late in 1791 and scheduled for publication
by Joseph Johnson at the price of a shilling a copy, was delayed and then
never was published, not because Johnson had lost faith in Blake's work
or wavered in support of revolution but because publishing such work
was becoming risky; the house of Joseph Priestly, a republican writer
whose work Johnson published, "was ransacked by a 'patriot' mob in
1791;" (Ackroyd 158) and the British government was prosecuting
radicals. Although he had begun to print Paine's *Rights of Man*, a
profitable venture considering how popular a book it was, Johnson
turned publication over to another printer in fear of such laws as the
1792 "Royal Proclamation against Divers Wicked Seditious Writings,"
(Bronowski 68) and because of near martial law indicated by the
presence of British and Prussian troops barracked around London.
(Ackroyd 156) Indeed, repression in England had become so serious that
a warrant for Paine's arrest was issued after he addressed the Friends of

the People in September 1792, and there is an unsubstantiated story that Blake saw him in Johnson's office and warned him of his ensuing arrest, spiriting him out of the place towards a ship at Dover just twenty minutes before the warrant for his arrest arrived. (Bronowski 68) In 1798, Joseph Johnson was arrested and imprisoned for six months for selling what was called a seditious pamphlet. (Ackroyd 181)

In this climate the surface content of Blake's poetry changed, moving to the mystifications of his complex mythology away from aphoristic assertions of political and spiritual ideas. Nevertheless, Blake maintained his political radicalism, but fearfully. In the same year Johnson was imprisoned, Blake wrote, "To defend the Bible in this year 1798 would cost a man his life[.] The Beast [the State]& the Whore [the Church] rule without controls.... I have been commanded from Hell [the center of active energy] not to Print this as it is what our Enemies wish." The government, he realized, would be only too glad to arrest him. Blake's defense of Paine and condemnation of Watson's tract were not published. (Ackroyd 182)

Blake devoted himself to his work. He developed a process of "direct color printing from copper plates;" (Ackroyd 182) he made a "uniform set of all his illuminated books on larger, folio-sized, paper" in 1795, (Ackroyd 191) and he worked at commissions he got from friends who were concerned that "poor Blake will not be out of need of money." (Ackroyd 182) In 1794, Flaxman returned to England from Italy and resumed his association with Blake, recommending him to employers and having him re-engrave some of his [Flaxman's] outlines of the *Odyssey* which had been lost at sea on his return to England. He also commissioned a series of engravings for the poems of Thomas Grey as a gift for Mrs. Flaxman. George Cumberland, another friend who had just returned from Italy, got Blake work engraving plates for a volume concerned with *The Antiquities of Athens* and for an aesthetic treatise of his own, *Thoughts on Outline*. (Ackroyd 182)

Blake's work was held in high regard. Cumberland wrote in his *Thoughts* that having Blake's engravings in the book was "a compliment from a man of ... extraordinary genius and abilities, the highest, I believe, I shall ever receive." (Ackroyd 182) But all the acclaim that came to him as a journeyman engraver from friends who were academicians like Richard Cosway, or international celebrities, like Flaxman, or published critics like Cumberland angered Blake as much as it delighted him. It signified once again how the recognition he truly desired for his imaginative and creative genius as a poet and as a painter had evaded him, while men whom he believed to be, and, in fact, who were his artistic inferiors, were enjoying recognition, exhibition, publication, and reputation. And while some of his commissioned projects had artistic merit, still he was doing other people's work, as when he engraved plates for Mrs. Flaxman of Robert Grey's poetry. Other projects were purely commercial, like engraving a map of Hafod, a district in North Wales, or a series of plates for carpet advertisements. "I live by Miracle," Blake wrote:

> as to Engraving, in which art I cannot reproach myself with any neglect, yet I am laid by in a comer as if I did not Exist, & Since my Young's Night Thoughts have been publish'd, Even Johnson & Fuseli have discarded my Graver. (Ackroyd 205)

Blake felt especially bitter towards Johnson because Johnson, according to Blake, had written to him discouraging him from continuing his own creative work. (Ackroyd 205) And times were bad in general for art. The war with France was draining money from England.

Towards the end of the 1790s, still concerned for Blake, Flaxman introduced Thomas Butts to him. Butts was a Swedenborgian, the chief clerk in the War Office, and he had accumulated a modest fortune because of the system of fees and patronage that government employees of the time enjoyed. He owned a grand house and speculated successfully in the stock and real estate markets. He became Blake's patron, providing Blake with modest but steady commissions over the next ten years. Of him, Samuel Palmer wrote, he "stood between the greatest designer in England and the workhouse." (Ackroyd 206) Butts' first commission was a series of "small Pictures from the Bible." Butts ordered fifty at a guinea each, "which," Blake wrote, "is Something better than mere copying after another artist." (Ackroyd 206)

Butts' patronage did not, however, alter Blake's circumstances or his temperament greatly. He continued to grow as an artist and adhere to his calling despite whatever setbacks and slights he encountered. He worked on a series of temperas for Butts and exhibited two of them, "The Last Supper," in 1799 and "The Miracle of the Loaves and Fishes," in 1800 at the Royal Academy, where he had not exhibited for fourteen years. Although he adhered to tempera, Blake had seen and been moved by exhibitions of European oils including works by Caravaggio, Veronese, Correggio, Raphael, Poussin, Titian, Michelangelo, and Tintoretto at several London galleries, and his work showed their painterly influence, especially in his use of perspective.

Temperamentally, Blake still appeared to be a man of strange religion to his friends. Butts in a letter told Blake that he was limited by "certain opinions imbib'd from reading, nourish'd by indulgence, and riveted by a confin'd Conversation." Blake's spiritual associates at this time, around 1800, were in fact political radicals, mesmerists, nudists, magicians, and people who were thought to take special drugs and elixirs and to practice erotic rituals. Butts himself is the source of one anecdote which gives a sense of Blake's sexual radicalism. The story is accepted as credible by Blake scholars:

> At the end of the little garden in Hercules Buildings [where the Blakes lived in Lambeth] there was a summer-house. Mr. Butts calling one day found Mr. and Mrs. Blake sitting in the summer-house, freed from "those troublesome disguises" which have prevailed since the Fall. "Come in!" cried Blake; "it's only Adam and Eve, you know!" [Blake] and wife had been reciting passages from *Paradise Lost*, in character, and the garden of Hercules Buildings [made] to represent the Garden of Eden. (Ackroyd 154)

Temperamentally, Blake was still capable of his old indignation and irascibility. George Cumberland, with the thought of doing Blake some good, introduced him to the Reverend John Trusler towards the end of the 1790s. Trusler was the author of such self-help tomes as *The Way to be Rich and Respectable* and *A Sure way to Lengthen Life*. Trusler commissioned Blake to do four watercolors for him, "Malevolence," "Benevolence," "Pride," and "Humility." After receiving "Malevolence," Trusler cancelled the commission and wrote to Blake complaining about the quality of the workmanship. Blake wrote back:

> I really am sorry that you are fall'n out with the Spiritual World.... You say that I want somebody to Elucidate my

Ideas. But you ought to know that What is Grand is
necessarily obscure to Weak men. That which can be made
Explicit to the Idiot is not worth my care. (Ackroyd 209)

AT FELPHAM IN SUSSEX, 1800–1803

I am really sorry to see my Countrymen trouble themselves
about Politics. If Men were Wise the Most arbitrary Princes
could not hurt them[.] If they are not Wise the freest
Government is compelld to be a Tyrrany[.] Princes appear to
me to be Fools[.] Houses of Commons & Houses of Lords
appear to me to be fools[. T]hey seem to me to be something
Else besides Human Life. (Ackroyd 160)

This is a very political abjuration of politics and it reflects a sense of
alienation and defeat Blake felt. By the year 1800, Blake still had to rely
on condescending patronage for his art. His poetry was hardly
recognized at all. England was deep in a war with France. Liberties of
expression and legal protections like *habeas corpus* were curtailed and
people were without food. In London there were bread riots. In such a
climate Blake's engraving business was not thriving.

In 1800, the Blakes left London and set up house in a cottage in
Felpham in Sussex belonging to William Hayley, who became Blake's
patron for the three years of his sojourn there. Twelve years Blake's
senior, his life had intersected Blake's several times before. Hayley had
lived next door to Basire's shop when Blake was his apprentice, and
Flaxman had sent Hayley a copy of Blake's *Poetical Sketches* along with
the condescending apology for them. His name all but unknown now,
Hayley was a popular poet and playwright in the late eighteenth-century.
He wrote treatises on painting and poetry, and he was the first English
translator of Dante's *Commedia*. He had been educated at Eton and
Cambridge. When his natural son, Thomas Alphonso, a sickly but
artistically gifted nineteen-year-old was dying, at Butts' suggestion,
Hayley commissioned Blake to engrave two of the young man's
drawings, one of Pericles, one of Demosthenes, as well as a medallion of
the young man's likeness for inclusion in his verse epistle, *An Essay on
Sculpture*. Blake's finished engraving of Thomas Alphonso did not satisfy
him or the dying boy and Blake revised his work without scolding him

as he had the Reverend Trusler, but the boy died before Blake had finished and Blake sent a warm letter of condolence and told of his own loss thirteen years earlier of his beloved brother, Robert.

At this time, perhaps the association of the death of Thomas Alphonso with Robert's death was a significant factor, but whatever the cause, which was a mystery to him, Blake experienced severe depression. He wrote that he fell into a "Deep pit of Melancholy, Melancholy without any real reason for it." (Ackroyd 215) At this time, too, just after his son's funeral, Hayley came to London to stay with friends at Kew, and he visited Blake and proposed that Blake return to Felpham in Sussex with him and work on another portrait of Thomas Alphonso. Blake agreed and once in Felpham further agreed to rent a small cottage there for twenty pounds a year from the landlord of the local inn and work, in Hayley's words, "under my auspices." Blake's cottage was small, but nevertheless there were two staircases in it, one at either end, and three rooms on each of the two floors. From the front window, there was a view beyond the garden and the cornfields of a sliver of the sea. Blake drew a sketch of the cottage with an angel hovering above it. The hint of condescending patronage in Hayley's phrase "under my auspices" was echoed and amplified in Flaxman's letter to Hayley, approving the arrangement:

I hope that Blake's residence at Felpham will be a Mutual Comfort to you & him, & I see no reason why he should not make as good a livelihood there as in London, if he engraves & teaches drawing ... as also by making neat drawings of different kinds[,] but if he places any dependence on painting large pictures, for which he is not qualified, either by habit or study, he will be miserably deceived. (Ackroyd 215, 6)

It was an assessment that Hayley had no trouble agreeing with. His patronage was benevolent, but he did not realize, as Flaxman did not, the quality of genius he was overlooking. Consequently his attitude towards Blake has a bitterly ironic quality. He suggested, once Blake was established in his cottage at Felpham and had begun working on projects for him that in order to augment his income, Blake ought to tutor some of the wealthier families of the area, and towards this end presumed to teach Blake the art of painting miniatures:

I have an excellent enthusiastic Creature, a Friend of
Flaxman, under my own Eye residing in this village; he is by
profession an Engraver, but he says I have taught Him to
paint in miniature, & in Truth He has improved his excellent
versatile Talents very much in this retired scene. (Ackroyd
221)

An excellent miniaturist already, Blake apparently subdued his spirit and
tolerated his subordination, at least for a while, and simply wrote Butts,
"Mr Hayley acts like a Prince." (221)

Blake began his stay at Felpham, despite his London depression, in
good cheer: "Our journey" of seventy miles, which took seventeen
hours, "was very pleasant ... No Grumbling, All was Cheerfulness &
Good Humor.... My fingers Emit sparks of fire with Expectations of my
future labors." (Ackroyd 217) Blake found the cottage "congenial to the
wants of Man," and, in Felpham, that, "Meat is cheaper than in London,
but the sweet air & the voices of winds, trees & birds, & the odours of
the happy ground, makes it a dwelling for immortals." (Ackroyd 218) In
Felpham, too "voices of Celestial inhabitants are more distinctly heard,
& their forms more distinctly seen, & my Cottage is also a Shadow of
their houses." (218)

It is possible to interpret Blake's cheerfulness as compensating for
the sense of loss he felt regarding earthly recognition for his proper
work, and as a strongly willed effort to keep bitterness at bay: he wrote
to Flaxman from Felpham at this time,

I am more famed in Heaven for my works than I could well
concieve. In my Brain are studies & Chambers fill'd with
books & pictures of old, which I wrote and painted in ages of
Eternity before my mortal life; & those works are the delight
& Study of Archangels. Why, then, should I be anxious about
the riches or fame of mortality.... I look back into the regions
of Reminiscence & behold our ancient days before this Earth
appear'd in its vegetated mortality to my mortal vegetated
Eyes. (Ackroyd 218)

At Felpham there was an abundance of commercial work and Blake
served more as a factotum than an artist. Hayley called him "*my*

secretary" and "the friendly Zealous Engraver who daily works by *my* side ... *my* worthy artist who works constantly in *my* study" (emphasis added). (Ackroyd 220, 2) Blake's first job was to illustrate "Little Tom the Sailor," a ballad Hayley wrote to commemorate the death at sea of the son of a poor Folkstone widow. Income from the sales of the poem was to go to the widow. On their wooden press, Catherine Blake printed the two etchings Blake had made. Following "Little Tom the Sailor," Blake did a series of heads including Homer, Dante, Chaucer, Tasso, Milton, Spenser, Shakespeare, Dryden, and Thomas Alphonso for Hayley's library. Hayley engaged Blake to do engravings for his *Life* of the poet, William Cowper, who had been a friend and who died mad, within a week of his son. Hayley also introduced Blake to the wealthy families of the area who employed him as a drawing teacher or commissioned him to paint miniatures. He was even asked "to paint a set of handscreens for a lady of quality." He declined. (Ackroyd 226)

Despite the condescension which was probably more a characteristic of his class than of his personality, Hayley seems to have liked Blake as much as he seems to have liked having him in his service. From a number of his letters, a sense of Blake in Felpham emerges. At work, Catherine was his assistant. She put the "empty [copper] plate," Blake was to engrave "upon the little round oak table." As he worked Blake was patient:

> Engraving, of all human Works, [Hayley wrote to a friend] appears to require the largest Portion of patience and he [Blake] happily possesses more of that inestimable Virtue, than I ever saw united before to an Imagination so lively & so prolific! (Ackroyd 224)

(Given his consciousness of how ill-used his genius was, Blake was in fact more patient than Hayley knew.) They went out riding together, Blake on a horse called Bruno. In Hayley's drawing room, Blake sang his poetry to an appreciative audience. Hayley also provided the fullest description of William and Catherine Blake as husband and wife. He wrote that Catherine was

> the only female on Earth, who could have suited Him ex*actly*. They have been married more than 17 years & are as fond of

each other if their Honey Moon were still shining—They live in a neat little cottage, which they both regard as the most delightful residence ever inhabited by a mortal; they have no servant:—the good woman not only does all the work of the House, but she even makes the greatest part of her Husbands dress, & assists him in *his art*—she draws, she engraves, & sings delightfully & is so truly the Half of her good man, that they seem animated by one Soul, & that a soul of indefatigable Industry & benevolence—it sometimes hurries them both to laour *rather too much*. (Ackroyd 232)

As far as Hayley could see, as he wrote in a letter to Flaxman,

our good Blake grows more & more attach'd to this pleasant marine village, & seems to gain in it a perpetual increase of improving Talents & settled Comfort. (Ackroyd 224)

Blake's sense of the situation, however, was different from Hayley's. He was depressed. About his work he wrote, "if it was fit for me, I doubt not that I should be Employ'd in Greater things." (Ackroyd 232) He was doing illustrations for Hayley's verse and doing engravings of designs made by Flaxman's wife. In November, he wrote to Butts that he was "very Unhappy." Perhaps desperately reassuring himself about his art, which was in advance of the ability of the people of his time to comprehend it, Blake wrote,

I have travel'd thro' Perils & Darkness not unlike a Champion. I have Conquer'd, and shall still Go on Conquering. Nothing can withstand the fury of my Course among the Stars of God & in the Abysses of the Accuser.... I am under the direction of Messengers from Heaven, daily & nightly. (Ackroyd 233)

He also had forebodings of "Spiritual Enemies of ... formidable magnitude." (233) At the beginning of 1803 Blake decided to return to London, for it was only there, he wrote Butts, that "I can ... carry on my visionary studies ... unannoy'd, & that I may converse with my friends in Eternity, See Visions, Dream Dreams & prophecy & speak Parables."

(Ackroyd 235) He could no longer tolerate Hayley whom he claimed was "jealous" of him,

> & will be no further My friend than he is compelled by circumstances. The truth is, as a Poet he is frighten'd at me & as a Painter his views & mine are opposite. (Ackroyd 233)

Whether Hayley was jealous of Blake or Blake expressed his own resentment of Hayley's unworthy fame and his own unjust neglect in such an accusation is a matter for speculation and less important than the actual situation, that the superior artist was serving the inferior one, that the inferior artist was in power and condescending and the superior one, in order to eat, had to be compliant. To Hayley, Blake's moments of self-assertion and rebellion were hardly comprehensible, as the following note he sent to Flaxman demonstrates:

> Blake surprized me a little in saying (after we had settled the price of 30 Guineas for the first, the price which He had for the Cowper) that Romney's head would require much Labor & he must have 40 for it—startled as I was I replied I will not stint you in behalf of Romney—you shall have 40— but soon after while we were looking at the smaller & slighter drawing of the Medallion He astonished me by saying I must have 30 G for this—I then replied—of this point I must consider. (Ackroyd 234)

It is not difficult to suppose that frequently Blake held his resentment and his anger in check for the sake of getting on in a world which was thwarting him. The ache this sort of necessity causes anyone is palpable. In the case of the poet who wrote, "Sooner murder an infant in its cradle than nurse unacted desires," it was very likely devastating and required such counter reflections as what Blake wrote to his brother James when he told him of his intention to return to London: " I know that the Public are my friends & love my works & will embrace them whenever they see them." (Ackroyd 235)

Perhaps the key to what troubled him in his benefactor's magnanimous condescension lies in Blake's idea of the benefits to be found in London. In London, he wrote, he would be "unobserv'd & at

liberty from the Doubts of other Mortals; perhaps Doubts proceeding
from kindness, but Doubts are always pernicious, Especially when we
Doubt our Friends." (Ackroyd 235) Blake's art was a result of the exercise
of the delicate faculty of visionary imagination and the strong
commitment to credit that faculty despite the scientism and skepticism
of his era. The enemy of such a position, indeed, is doubt, which if it
infects the artist's sensibility can destroy his entire artistic capability. In
"Auguries of Innocence," Blake had expressed his fear in cosmic term:

> If the Sun & Moon should Doubt
> Theyd immediately Go out.

That Blake accurately judged Hayley to be "much averse to my
poetry," renders him therefore a potentially harmful acquaintance. Blake
wrote to Butts with a renewed sense of his own strength:

> I would not send you a Drawing or a Picture till I had again
> reconsider'd my notions of Art & had put myself back as if I
> was a learner.

and of the rightness of his art:

> I have now given two years to the intense study of those parts
> of the art which relate to light & shade & colour, & am
> Convinc'd that either my understanding is incapable of
> comprehending the beauties of Colouring, or the pictures
> which I painted for you Are Equal in Every part of Art, &
> superior in One, to any thing that has been done since the
> age of Rafael. (Ackroyd 241)

To his brother, he wrote with optimism about publishing his own works:

> The Profits arising from Publications are immense, & I now
> have it in my power to commence publication with many
> very formidable works, which I have finish'd & ready.
> (Ackroyd 236)

Before Blake returned to London, however, the aggressive

paranoia of militaristic patriotism confronted him in the form of a drunken soldier in his garden, and Blake found himself in the wearisome and frightening position of having to defend himself against charges of sedition before an English magistrate. There was great fear in England, in 1803, that Napoleon's fleet would invade. Soldiers were deployed throughout the Sussex countryside and some, like John Scofield of the First Regiment of Dragoons, were billeted at the Fox Inn in Felpham.

What is known for sure is that *something* happened between Blake and Scofield in Blake's garden on August 12, 1803, that it resulted in Scofield's complaint, Blake's trial, and Blake's subsequent acquittal. Precisely what that something was can only be reconstructed from the testimonies of Blake and Scofield, which differ widely from each other. According to Blake upon finding Scofield, who was a stranger to him, in his garden, he asked him to leave. Scofield

> made me an impertinent answer. I insisted on his leaving the Garden; he refused. I still persisted in desiring his departure; he then threaten'd to knock out my Eyes, with many abominable imprecations & with some contempt for my Person; it affronted my foolish Pride. I therefore took him by the Elbows & pushed him before me till I had got him out; there I intended to have left him, but he, turning about, put himself into a Posture of Defiance, threatening & swearing at me. I, perhaps foolishly & perhaps not, stepped out at the Gate, &, putting aside his blows, took him again by the Elbows, &, keeping his back to me, pushed him forwards down the road about fifty yards—he all the while endeavouring to turn round & strike me, & raging & cursing, which drew out several neighbours. (Ackroyd 245)

According to Scofield, Blake accosted him in the garden declaring that

> The People of England were like a Parcel of Children, that they would play with themselves till they got scalded and burnt, that the French knew our Strength very well, and if Bonaparte should come he would be master of Europe in an Hour's Time, that England might depend on it, that when he set his Foot on English Ground that every Englishman

would have his choice, whether to have his Throat cut, or to
join the French, & that he [Blake] was a strong Man, and
would certainly begin to cut Throats, and the strongest Man
must conquer—that he damned the King of England—his
Country, & his Subjects, that his Soldiers were all bound for
Slaves, and all the Poor People in general.

Scofield implicated Catherine, too, testifying that she came out of the
cottage saying that 'the King of England would run him Into the Fire,
that he might [not] get himself out again. & altho' she was but a Woman,
she would fight for as long as she had a drop of Blood in her," that she
"would not fight against France but "would for Bonaparte as long as I am
able." Scofield concluded by saying that Blake repeatedly said "Damn
the King. The soldiers are all slaves." (Ackroyd 244, 5)

The incident concluded with Blake delivering the soldier with his
hands pinned behind his back to the inn where the innkeeper persuaded
him to go inside. Blake believed that the charge of sedition was cooked
up by Scofield and another soldier in order to have revenge on him.
None of the witnesses, neither his gardener nor any of the neighbors
who were drawn into the street by the altercation had heard Blake say
anything Scofield had accused him of saying. Despite the fortunate
outcome of the trial—after but an hour Blake was acquitted to applause
and "an uproar of noisy exultations" (Ackroyd 251)—being arrested put
Blake under a cloud of dread for months. Although free on bail, put up
by Hayley, he was unnerved. He suspected he was the victim of a
government plot because he had been an associate of radicals like Tom
Paine and Mary Wollstonecraft. He sometimes even suspected that
Hayley might have been involved, which seems unlikely—just as it is
unlikely that the presiding magistrate knew anything of Blake's former
associations, for that would have told badly against him. It is possible,
however, although there is no way of knowing, that Blake had said some
of the things Scofield accused him of having said or near variants. He
was prone to temper and he was, after all, the poet who believed, "war is
energy Enslav'd." (Ackroyd 250)

BACK IN LONDON

With his return to London, what Blake called a period of darkness ended: twenty years of working as a commercial engraver and an artist on other people's projects. But Blake did not like London as he found it in 1804: "in London every calumny And falsehood utter'd against another of the same trade is thought fair play.... we are not in a field of battle, but in a City of Assassinations." (Ackroyd 256) He had few commissions, even from his friends, who frequently used other engravers. Besides what they might have seen as his peculiarities of temperament and temper, they also found that Blake was a slow workman. Hayley suffered "Consternation" that "was *extereme*" when etchings Blake was to have sent "were not arriv'd ... at the Cottage on *Friday*." (Ackroyd 255) Blake's response was Delphic:

> I am going on briskly with the plates & if God blesses me with health doubt not yet to make a Figure in the Great Dance of Life that shall amuse the Spectators in the Sky. (Ackroyd 255)

Blake may have been referring to other work than Hayley's, art he hoped would "amuse the Spectators in the Sky," his proper audience, the one which valued his true talent. In any event, Hayley's plates were not ready for yet another year. But Blake needed money nonetheless and it made him a suppliant. Supplication sometimes took the form of the self-assertion that so surprised Hayley, but it often took a self-effacing form, and there are a number of letters from Blake to Hayley in which Blake defers to his judgment on various aesthetic matters and begs him for money. Undoubtedly, his appreciation of Hayley's support during his trial is sincere:

> Gratitude is Heaven itself; there could be no heaven without Gratitude. I feel it & I know it. I thank God & Man for it & above all You, My dear friend & benefactor in the Lord. (Ackroyd 254)

The strength of Blake's poetic inspiration seems to have been derived from the very conditions which provoked his despair: his isolation as an artist, his humiliation as a craftsman. The nature of his visionary work in poetry and painting equally reflects criticism and transcendence of oppressive circumstances, which he saw as systemic.

Alienated as he was, however, from his contemporaries he was one in spirit with the great masters and his association was with them. In 1804 he attended several exhibitions of European painting Count Truchsess, bankrupt by the French revolution, had brought to England, and the experience restored his sense of himself as an artist:

> I was again enlightened with the light I enjoyed in my youth, and which has for exactly twenty years been closed from me as by a door and by window-shutters.... [E]xcuse my enthusiasm or rather madness, for I am really drunk with intellectual vision whenever I take a pencil or graver into my hand, even as I used to be in my youth, and as I have not been for twenty dark, but very profitable years. I thank God that I courageously pursued my course through darkness. (Ackroyd 256)

The result was that Blake did no commercial engraving for the next eleven years, having found "the courage to suffer poverty and disgrace" (Ackroyd 258) as he "Convers[ed] with Eternal Realities as they Exist in the Human Imagination[.]" His credo remained what it always had been, an opposition to a materialist view of nature and to belief in fluctuation and mutability: "We are in a World of Generation & death & this world we must cast off if we would be Painters." (Ackroyd 258) This was not only an aesthetic belief. It was the statement of a spiritual creed:

> These States Exist now[.] Man Passes on but States remain for Ever[. H]e passes thro them like a traveller who may as well suppose that the places he has passed thro exist no more as a Man may suppose that the States he has passed thro exist no more[.] Every Thing is Eternal. (Ackroyd 279)

In 1804, Blake began engraving the images and writing the text for his epics, *Milton* and *Jerusalem*.

Although Blake had stopped doing commercial engraving and was "as much myself when I take the Pencil or Graver into my hand as I used to be in my youth," (Ackroyd 258) he did not, could not, because of his need for money, give up all commercial projects. Indeed, he had no tolerance for an argument that want nurtured art. "[W]orks of Art,"

Blake wrote, "can only be produced in Perfection where the Man is either in Affluence or is Above the Care of it." (Ackroyd 265) He did engravings of his own designs for a volume of Hayley's *Ballads*, from which, it was agreed, he was to earn royalties on sales, but the edition did not do well. Blake also hoped to do engravings for Hayley's *Life* of the eighteenth-century English portrait painter, George Romney, but Hayley's regard for Blake's work had declined, as his note to Lady Hesketh accompanying his *Ballads* makes plain. He notes that Blake's work shows *"more Zeal* than *Success,"* and asks her to

> smile on [Blake's] gratitude tho you will frown on some productions of his pencil, particularly *the last*, in the little volume, which He thinks the best—so little can artists & authors judge of their own recent Composition. (Ackroyd 263)

Although Blake lost Hayley's patronage, Thomas Butts remained loyal to him and for the next five years commissioned works from him and supplied him with a steady, if modest, income.

There was a disturbing and recurring pattern, however. Friends thought highly of Blake and offered him work but then withdrew the commission because they found his work "wild." One such instance concerns a volume of lugubrious poetry called *The Grave*, for which Robert Hartley Cromek, an engraver turned publisher, asked Blake to engrave illustrations of his own [Blake's] making for the volume. Cromek and his associates liked Blake's illustrations, but disliked Blake's subsequent engravings of the illustrations and gave the work to another engraver, Luigi Schiavonetti. Blake was disappointed. He saw his removal from the project as one more event in a lifelong pattern of rejection. But he was given credit in the volume for the original designs from which the engravings were made. Indeed, Cromek commissioned Thomas Phillips to paint Blake's portrait and Schiavonetti to engrave it for a frontispiece. Perhaps the tribute was partially mitigated by "a wildness in the eye" that a reviewer saw in the picture.

Through Cromek's recommendation, too, Blake was asked to design the frontispiece, a picture of the dead child, for Benjamin Malkin's *A Father's Memoir of his Child*. After seeing it, however, Cromek erased Blake's work and drew the portrait himself. But in this volume, there appears the first printed account of Blake's early life. Malkin refers to Blake's "warm and brilliant imagination," and he characterizes Blake's detractors quite as Blake himself would:

> By them have the higher powers of this artist been kept from public notice, and his genius tied down, as far as possible, to the mechanical department of his profession. By them, in short, has he been stigmatised as an engraver, who might do tolerably well, if he was not mad. (Ackroyd 268)

And Cromek, whom Blake thought of as "a Petty sneaking Knave" and a "Cheat," (Ackroyd 270) wrote of Blake, that his drawings

> claim approbation, sometimes excite our wonder, and not seldom our fears, when we see him play on the very verge of legitimate invention; but wildness so picturesque in itself, so often redeemed by taste, simplicity and elegance, what child of fancy, what artist would wish to discharge ? (Ackroyd 268)

Blake was an anomaly to the artists and publishers who were his contemporaries and who tried to provide work for him, because his productions were so completely his own and often out of step with contemporary fashion, and thus lacking in commercial profitability. What often seems like condescension by contemporaries may be perplexity. Not blessed with Blake's vision, they were at a loss when their attempts to help him, they felt, could only hinder their own business. He appeared mad and wild. Here is Cromek, in a letter to Blake, expressing anger and frustration:

> I neither have, nor ever had, any encouragement from you to place you before the public in a more favourable point of view.... I had to battle with a man who had pre-determined not to be served. What public reputation you have, the reputation of eccentricity excepted, I have acquired for you.... I believed what you so often have told me, that your works were equal, nay superior, to a Raphael or to a Michael Angelo!... I have imposed on myself yet more grossly in believing you to be one altogether abstracted from this

world, holding converse with the world of spirits! (Ackroyd 272, 273)

Visionary Blake, focused on his art rather than the realities which might hinder it, was in no position, either, to understand their frustration or to compromise his vision or his labor. Instead, he sometimes became resentful and combative. But that reaction was productive. When Cromek commissioned Thomas Stothard to paint a scene from Chaucer of the Canterbury pilgrims, Blake in anger that the idea had been his first, painted and engraved the scene, too, and produced a work of grandeur and precision.

Amidst conflicts, disappointments, and poverty, while doing work for hire, Blake kept doing his own work as poet and painter. In 1809 he exhibited. The exhibition was completely a failure. The one review of it, in *The Examiner* dismissed Blake as an "unfortunate lunatic, whose personal inoffensiveness secures him from confinement." Indeed, the leaflet Blake composed to announce the exhibit will not serve as a model for any student of public relations, except perhaps of what not to do:

> The ignorant Insults of individuals will not hinder me from doing my duty to my Art.... those who have been told that my Works are but an unscientific and irregular Eccentricity, a Madman's Scrawls, I demand of them to do me the justice to examine before they decide.... if Art is the glory of a Nation, if Genius and Inspiration are the great Origin and bond of Society, the distinction my Works have obtained ... calls for my Exhibition as the greatest of Duties to my country. (Ackroyd 285)

The catalogue Blake assembled to accompany the exhibit, the critic wrote, represented "the wild ebullitions of a distempered brain." (Ackroyd 289) It expressed Blake's anger at his exclusion from the ranks of the artists and was written

> in self-defense against the insolent and envious imputation of unfitness for finished and scientific art; and this imputation, most artfully and industriously endeavored to be propagated among the public by ignorant hirelings.... to be left and

neglected, and [my] work ... cried down as eccentricity and madness; as unfinished and neglected by the artist's violent temper. (Ackroyd 287)

Around this time, too, Blake read through the works of Joshua Reynolds, the celebrated painter whom he had detested for the blurry gentility of his work since his days at the Academy. Blake's annotation of Reynold's *Works* reaffirms his distaste for Reynold's and his influence. "This Man was Hired to Depress Art," Blake wrote on the front page and continued:

> Having spent the Vigour of my Youth and Genius under the Oppression of Sr Joshua & his Gang of Cunning Hired Knaves Without Employment & as much as could possibly be Without Bread, The Reader must Expect to Read in all my Remarks on these Books Nothing but Indignation & Resentment While Sr Joshua was rolling in Riches Barry was Poor & Unemployd except by his own Energy Mortimer was called a Madman & only Portrait Painting applauded & rewarded by the Rich & Great. Reynolds & Gainsborough Blotted & Blurred one against the other & Divided all the English World between them.... I was hid.... I am hid. (Ackroyd 284)

A PROPHET HONORED IN HIS OWN TIME

Although Blake made no secret of his resentment for the way he and his work were dismissed, his primary response to his calumniators was to continue to work, to retain his capacity to see visions and to translate them into art. He did paintings and engravings of scenes from Milton's poetry, the *Book of Job*, Dante's *Divine Comedy*, and a monumental rendition of the Last Judgment, a complexly wrought work with more than a thousand figures, looking like a stone carving for a cathedral. He worked on his epics, *Milton* and *Jerusalem*. He taught himself Italian and Hebrew. And while Blake was reputed among his contemporaries to be a poor madmen and while he had less and less contact with them because of his stormy temper (Ackroyd 327), their disdain, and because death began its winnowing, he slowly became a figure of regard and admiration for a younger generation who chose him over his contemporaries. Seymour Kirkup, met Blake around 1810, and later described his impression:

> His high qualities I did not prize at that time; besides, I thought him mad. I do not think so now. I never suspected him of imposture. His manner was too honest for that. He was very kind to me, though very positive in his opinion, with which I never agreed. (Ackroyd 295)

In 1815, the son of Blake's friend from his days at the Royal Academy, George Cumberland visited the Blakes and "found him & his wife drinking Tea durtyer than ever." But conversation with Blake often left the interlocutor with an odd but favorable impression. Charlotte Bury, after meeting Blake at a dinner given by Caroline Lamb at the beginning of 1818 wrote in her diary:

> Mr Blake appears unlearned in all that concerns this world, and from what he said, I should fear that he was one of those whose feelings are far superior to his station in life. He looks care-worn and subdued; but his countenance radiated as he spoke of his favourite pursuit, and he appeared gratified by talking to a person who comprehended his feelings. I can easily imagine that he seldom meets with any one who enter views; for they are peculiar, and exalted above the common level of received opinions. (Ackroyd 323)

But that was changing. In 1818, Cumberland's son visited Blake and brought with him John Linnell, the son of a London carver, gilder and print seller, a painter himself, an admirer of Michelangelo, strong in his opinions, and like Blake, five feet five inches tall. Although much younger than Blake, he became a patron and a close friend. "We soon became intimate," Linnell wrote in an unpublished autobiography, "& I employed him to help me with an engraving of my portrait of Mr Upton a Baptist preacher which he was glad to do having scarcely enough employment to live by at the prices he could obtain." But Linnell did much more than that. He introduced Blake to a number of the titled aristocracy in order to "get him some work." He regularly supported him with gifts of money, presumably on account for work to be done. (Ackroyd 328) They went to art galleries together, and to the opera and the theater, where it is recorded they saw a production of *Oedipus Rex*. (Ackroyd 324) Linnell also recorded Blake's character and opinions at this time. They were as they always had been:

> I soon encountered Blake[']s peculiarities, and [was] somewhat taken aback by the boldness of some of his assertions. I never saw anything the least like madness ... I generally met with a sufficiently rational explanation in the most really friendly & conciliatory tone.... With all the admiration possible it must be confessed that [Blake] said many things tending to the corruption of Christian morals, even when unprovoked by controversy, and when opposed by the superstitious, the crafty, or the proud, he outraged all common sense and rationality by the opinions he advanced, occasionally indulging in the support of the most lax interpretations of the precepts of the Scripture. (Ackroyd 325)

Henry Crabb Robinson was another young man who recorded Blake's conversation in his last years:

> Christ he said—he is the only God—But then he added— And so am I and so are you. [But Christ] was wrong in suffering himself to be crucified. (Ackroyd 325)

Linnell was a fine engraver, who employed methods in his art congenial to Blake's aesthetic, and his presence seems to have stimulated and reinvigorated Blake's work. Blake's later style is lighter, freer, less formal, more delicate than his previous work. In addition, he reprinted copies of old works like the *Songs of Innocence and Experience*, *The Marriage of Heaven and Hell*, and *The Book of Urizen*, often re-inking and re-coloring them in vibrant colors different from the originals. Because of a commission from Linnell, too, Blake did his Job series. Despite Linnell's contributions, Blake was still extremely poor, and Linnell got the members of the Royal Academy to grant him twenty-five pounds. He also took Blake to see the successful portrait painter, Thomas Lawrence, who soon after sent Blake a hundred pounds. (Ackroyd 343)

Linnell's care of Blake in his last years extended beyond providing him with financial help and inspiring new work. Linnell introduced Blake to Samuel Palmer. Palmer was nineteen when he met Blake, mystic in his religious belief, interested in medievalism and sacred art, and one of a group of young men, Edward Calvert, George Richmond, Francis Finch, Frederick Tatham, and John Giles, like himself, pious, mystic, even visionary, who called themselves The Ancients because they believed that the ancients were superior to the moderns in their sensibilities and the way they lived. The motto of their association was "Poetry and Sentiment." They wore long cloaks, went for excursions in the woods where they recited Virgil, sat up on camp-stools to watch the sun rise, improvised tragedies, and wandered through thunderstorms singing. When they spent a night in Bromley Churchyard in order to meditate, they were mistaken for grave-robbers. (Ackroyd 338) They idolized Blake and formed their circle around him, a lucrative trade at the time.

Giles called him "divine Blake," and when speaking of him to others said, he [Blake] "had seen God ... and had talked with angels." Richmond, who was fifteen when he met Blake said that taking a walk with Blake was like "walking with the prophet Isaiah." To these young men Blake was "approachable, kind and natural." Palmer wrote that Blake "had great powers of argument, and on general subjects was a very patient and good-tempered disputant; but materialism was his abhorrence; and if some un-happy man called in question the world of spirits, he would answer him 'according to his folly' by putting forth his own views in their most extravagant and startling aspect." (Ackroyd 340) Blake had found the future in which he had always believed in these young men's devotion to him and his work, and it was their written memoirs that helped bring Blake and his work into the present.

The last years of his life, Blake and Catherine lived on Fountain Street in London, and Blake had an extended set of admirers in The Ancients and was welcomed into their newly growing families with reverence and affection. Linnell had moved to Hampstead, and Blake visited him and his family on Sundays, walking from Fountain Court because he found riding in the Hampstead carriage sickened his stomach. The Linnell children waited on the road to greet him. Linnell painted a picture of Blake standing among the hills in a broad-brimmed Quaker-style hat. Blake played with the children. Sitting them on his lap he told them stories of his vision of a fold of lambs which turned out to be statuary, of clouds, of his affection for kittens, how he had once drunk the walnut oil he had intended to use for mixing colors, and he drew grasshoppers with them. In later years they remembered him as "a grave and sedate gentleman, with white hair, a lofty brow, and large lambent eyes [and of] a kind and gentle manner." (Ackroyd 361)

Blake paid similar visits to Palmer's and Calvert's families. He worked on an exquisitely colored copy of *Jerusalem*, on his Dante watercolors, on the canvass of *The Last Judgment*, which is now lost—the engraving survives—and on other engravings, which at last were being bought. But over the last several years of his life, he was often ill with chills, fevers, and stomach and bowel ailments. Blake died on August 12, 1827 of complications from gall stones. Linnell drew Blake's picture a few days before his death. On the twelfth, Blake lay in bed with Catherine at his bedside in tears. "Stay, Kate!" Blake said to his wife. "Keep just as you are—I will draw your portrait—for you have ever been an angel to me." Then he sang to her songs she later called "songs of joy and Triumph." In a letter to Samuel Palmer, George Richmond, who had been present and closed Blake's eyes "To keep the vision in" described Blake's death:

> He died on Sunday night at 6 Oclock in a most glorious manner. He said He was going to that Country he had all his life wished to see & expressed Himself Happy, hoping for Salvation through Jesus Christ—Just before he died his Countenance became fair. His eyes Brighten'd and He burst Singing of the things he saw in Heaven. (Ackroyd 367)

Blake was buried near his parents in the Dissenters' cemetery in Bunhill Fields on his forty-fifth wedding anniversary. Linnell paid for the service, and the members of The Ancients were present. Catherine died four years later in October 1831, "repeating texts of scripture and calling continually to her William, as if he were only in the next room, to say she was coming to him, and would not be long now."(Ackroyd 368) She was buried in Bunhill Fields.

WORKS CITED

Ackroyd, Peter. *Blake*. London: Sinclair-Stevenson, 1995, 399 p.

Brownowski, J. *William Blake*. Harmondsworth, Middlesex: Penguin Books, 1944, 218 p.

Erdman, David V., ed. The Poetry and Prose of William Blake. Commentary by Harold Bloom. Garden City, NY: Doubleday & Company, 1970. 908 p.

King, James. *William Blake: His Life*. London: Weidenfeld and Nicolson, 1991, 263 p.

Lister, Raymond. *William Blake: An Introduction to the Man and to His Work*. London: G. Bell and Sons, Ltd., 1968, 200 p.

Ruskin, John. "The Nature of Gothic." In *The Stones of Florence*. In *The Genius of John Ruskin*, John D. Rosenberg, ed. Boston: Houghton Mifflin Company, The Riverside Press, 1965, 560 p.

HEATHER DUBNICK

The Poet as Prophet:
William Blake, 1757–1827

William Blake occupies a unique place in the history of literature and art. He was a visionary, an artist, and a self-proclaimed prophet who challenged the literary conventions of his time. His unusual approach to poetry is noted even in anthologies and histories of literature, which usually characterize him as an early and somewhat marginal English Romantic poet. While he shared with other Romantic poets an interest in the imagination, a distaste for current neoclassical conventions, and a preference for ordinary, as opposed to ornate, poetic language, Blake clearly stands apart from later Romantic poets in many ways. Although his ideas are generally in sympathy with those of other Romantic poets, his work is truly unique in its style, attitude, and approach. To some extent, his separation from other Romantic poets was a function of time. His birth preceded those of William Wordsworth and Samuel Taylor Coleridge by more than a decade. Although other Romantic poets were well schooled in literature, Blake was self-educated to a great extent. His early education was also unique: while he was formally educated as an engraver, his literary knowledge resulted largely from his own reading and study. While he was well acquainted with the Bible, Milton, Dante, and the literary canon of the time, he was also exposed to a number of unconventional religious streams that had an immense influence on the development of his own religious theology.

Blake was both an artist and a poet, and this also sets him apart from other Romantic poets. Trained as an engraver, Blake, with the help of his wife Catherine, illustrated, illuminated, printed, and distributed his work himself. While his decision to publish his own works gave him complete control over their production, his method of printing was incredibly time-consuming. He could only produce a relatively small number of copies of each work, and as a result his audience necessarily remained quite small compared to that of other Romantic poets, who enjoyed the benefits of an expanded, literate audience.[1] Hence, Blake's work remained relatively unknown in his day, although his *Songs of Innocence and Experience* did attract the attention of Wordsworth, Coleridge, and others.[2]

Another consequence of Blake's decision to publish his own works was the variation and lack of standardization among editions. As a result, much of Blake's work was subject to revision, and as readers we have access to works at different stages of completion. In fact, many Blake scholars have pointed out that for this and other reasons Blake's poetry provides the student with an excellent lesson in poetry in general.[3]

While Blake received relatively little attention during his lifetime, during the Victorian Era his *Marriage of Heaven and Hell*—and Blake himself—began to receive renewed attention. Later poets, including Dante Gabriel Rossetti, Algernon Charles Swinburne, and William Butler Yeats, contributed to the recovery of Blake's position in the English literary canon. Critics such as Northrop Frye and David V. Erdman have rescued Blake from obscurity by illuminating within his work an entire aesthetic theory and an engagement with the politics of his time.[4] After much critical study and attention, Blake is today appreciated as an important poet with a unique approach to his art.

IMAGES AND WORDS

Blake's originality is evident in his engraving as well as in his poetry. Though Blake is better known as a poet, he played an important role in the history of art and printing as well. He developed a method of illuminated printing in which he simultaneously printed word and image through monochrome relief etching. Applying acid-resistant medium with pens and brushes, Blake wrote text in reverse on copper plates, drew the accompanying images, and then placed the plates in acid, which ate away any part of the plate not protected by the acid-resistant medium. He and his wife Catherine then would add the color by hand with a water-based medium. In their original form, each of Blake's books was a unique multimedia work of craft and artistry, inviting comparison with medieval illuminated manuscripts.

While some have attempted to study Blake's texts and images separately, Blake clearly meant them to be published and read together, and any reading based solely on the texts will necessarily be incomplete. The images do not merely illustrate or decorate the texts; they also contribute to a complete understanding of the meaning of Blake's words, sometimes by reinforcing the meaning of the text, other times by ironizing or challenging it.[5]

BLAKE'S VISION

Through this complex combination of words and images, Blake created an extensive mythology or theology. Blake's poetry revolves around the role of poet as visionary or prophet. As his character Los, the poet-prophet, famously says in *Jerusalem*, "I must Create a System or be enslaved by another Man's" (*Jerusalem* 20; Blake 316). Thus, Blake expresses the idea that the creation of a personal mythology is an act of resistance against received ideas. Blake's works weave together a variety of religious and mythological traditions, and readers often find his later prophecies quite difficult to follow. Many readers attempt to undertake the great labor of deciphering Blake's symbolism and paring it down to a simple allegoric system, but Blake's own focus on process and transformation resists such attempts. However fascinating the attempts to decipher Blake's symbolism, the large, unspoken message of Blake's prophecies is that the imagination of the individual poet is elevated to such a high plane, suggesting that it corresponds in importance to the myths, allegories, and symbols of established religions and churches. This is indeed a revolutionary position that reflects the sensibility of Romanticism.

Blake viewed the universe as dynamic and in constant flux. Many of his ideas evolved from his exposure to unconventional religious views, such as gnosticism and kabbalism, and unconventional thinkers, such as Emanuel Swedenborg and Jacob Boehme. These diverse views all share one aspect: the assertion of the non-rational as being as important as the rational, if not more so, emphasizing mysticism and intuitive knowledge, and elaborate systems of symbols. Blake argued against two camps that were themselves already at war: institutionalized religion and

Enlightenment philosophy. Religious institutions emphasized authority and rules, and Enlightenment philosophy emphasized rational thought. Blake felt that both should be subservient to intuition and imagination. He had an irreverent view of institutional religion, and he believed that official religion always places its own self-preservation above all. As a result, Blake's works constantly satirize and critique the Church and its teachings. Much of Blake's work is dedicated to his attempting to releasing the spirit of Jesus's teachings from the grip of the Church. At the same time, Blake disliked the Deist notions held by Enlightenment thinkers of a remote deity as first cause. In both cases, Blake argued against the distance between man and his creator, and proposed instead that "Man is All Imagination God is Man & exists in us & we in him" ("On George Berkeley," Blake 444). Suggesting an equivalence between God and man, Blake privileges the image of God incarnate in man—that is, Jesus—over more abstract ideas of God as a first cause or as a distant father-figure. By suggesting that God is man and in man, and also that "Man is All Imagination", Blake asserts a key idea of the Romantic sensibility—the primacy of imagination, emotion, and intuition. Blake refers to the empty, impersonal, conventional image of God as "Nobodaddy"; in his later prophetic work this role is represented by the character Urizen. Other authors may have held similar views, but Blake's forthright expression of these ideas makes him seem quite radical in comparison to other Romantic poets.

Man is at the center of Blake's universe. In Blake's view, all men are artists, and nature exists to be formed by man into civilization (Frye, *Fearful Symmetry*, 39). As poet and visionary, Blake understood his goal to be releasing others from the "mind-forg'd manacles" (Blake 53) imposed by convention so that they could recover their own vision of the true nature of things. The idea that all men are artists is an affirmation of the value of the individual and lies at the foundation of Blake's assertion of himself as a prophet.

Blake's universe is organized around the struggle between opposing forces. These forces create tension within individuals, within families, within societies, and among nations. In *The Marriage of Heaven and Hell*, Blake suggests that progress can only occur through the struggle between theses "Contraries":

Without Contraries is no progression. Attraction and

Repulsion, Reason and Energy, Love and Hate, are
necessary to Human existence. (86)

The goal for Blake is not resolution; the tension between
contraries is a necessity. While Blake's views suggest a dialectical view of
the universe, synthesis is never reached; the dynamism arising from the
tension between opposites is itself important and must be sustained.[6]

Blake's visions of apocalyptic struggle stem in part from the fact
that he lived in a time of immense political upheaval, most notably the
American and French Revolutions. Initially, Blake believed that these
revolutionary movements might be a sign of true, apocalyptic change in
the human condition, but he soon became disillusioned, particularly
with the events of the French Revolution, as he saw one tyrannical
system eventually replacing another.[7] As a man of visionary bent, he
truly expected the sort of visionary change suggested by the term
apocalypse, and took the hopes of revolutionary change quite literally.

Blake was himself a revolutionary in his own way; as Frye has
pointed out, Blake created a revolutionary structure of poetic imagery
(Frye, "Keys" 46–47). While earlier poets adhered to a view of the
universe in which fallen man, through his deeds, could either raise
himself toward Eden or lower himself into the world of mortality and
sin, Blake saw the universe in terms of two states, innocence and
experience. (These two states can be seen to correspond to the state of
Adam before and after the Fall, and hence, echo the ideas of gnosticism.)
Frye tells us that "[i]n place of the old construct [...] in which man
regains his happy garden home by doing his duty and obeying the law,
we have an uneasy revolutionary conception of conscious values and
standards of reality sitting on top of a volcano of thwarted and mainly
sexual energy" (47). As Frye points out, this "construct" can be seen
operating on two levels throughout Blake's work: individual/
psychological and social/political (47). Blake was revolutionary in his
time for his attempt to connect (or reconnect) spirituality and sexuality,
which had been strictly separated by organized religion for centuries.

Blake's poetry dramatizes all at once the struggle for sexual,
psychological, and political freedom. The desire for these freedoms
appears in the work of other Romantic poets, but in his expression of
that struggle, particularly in terms of sexual and psychological freedom,
Blake is far more direct and radical. The strength of the struggle is

expressed in Blake's poetry, which must be understood as dialogic or dialectical; the voices that inhabit his works cannot be taken to represent a single lyric voice, but rather they play out the interchange between various voices and perspectives.

FALL AND REDEMPTION

Blake's understanding of the world and of the role of the poet/prophet can best be understood in terms of Fall and Redemption. Blake believed strongly in the redemptive power of creativity to reunify a world fallen into contraries and oppositions. The role of the poet and the artist, for Blake, was to restore man to a previous state in which he would no longer be alienated from the world around him. (This may reflect Blake's interest in Gnosticism, which focuses intense interest in the innocent Adam before the Fall.) In this sense, both Fall and Redemption can be understood as psychological states.

Imagination, for Blake, is the key to man's redemption. In 1799, Blake wrote a famous letter defending the imagination to the Reverend Doctor John Trusler, who had criticized Blake's paintings of Malevolence and Benevolence. In this letter, Blake responds to Trusler:

> To the Eyes of a Miser a Guinea is more beautiful than the Sun, & a bag worn with the use of Money has more beautiful proportions than a Vine filled with Grapes. The tree which moves some to tears of joy is in the Eyes of others only a Green thing that stands in the way. Some See Nature all Ridicule & Deformity, & by these I shall not regulate my proportions; & Some Scarce see Nature at all. But to the Eyes of the Man of Imagination, Nature is Imagination itself. (Blake 448–49)

This passage makes clear Blake's view of the imagination and of the poet-prophet. Blake defined himself as a visionary, which for him meant someone with greater vision than the ordinary man. Blake believed that imagination could bring redemption to man's divided soul, and he understood his role as poet and painter to be that of sharing his vision and expanding the vision of others.

EARLY POETRY AND PROSE

Critics often divide Blake's works into the poetry and the prophecies. We can see pairs of contraries at work even in Blake's earliest works, such as the seasonal poems in *Poetical Sketches* (1783), a collection that overall displays both Blake's originality and his mastery of various poetic forms—from ballad to dramatic verse—at an early age (Eaves 191). The personification that Blake employs in these odes to the seasons hints at the elaborate cast of characters he will develop in his later work (Blake 3, n. 3).

In 1788, Blake published two illustrated tracts, *All Religions Are One* and *There is No Natural Religion*. The titles of these works alone express the challenge of Blake's ideas to established religion, and it is interesting that Blake chose to present these works as illustrated tracts, a form used for religious texts. The unsigned series *All Religions Are One* present Blake's concept of "Poetic Genius," which inhabits all men, while *There is No Natural Religion* presents Blake's critique of the Enlightenment worship of reason. Together, these two works contain the kernels of the principles implicit throughout Blake's later works.

SONGS OF INNOCENCE AND EXPERIENCE

Songs of Innocence, initially published in 1789 and later republished with *Songs of Experience*, focuses on the innocence and goodness of childhood as the ideal state of humanity. The poems were written during a time when Blake was particularly influenced by the works of Emanuel Swedenborg, a Swedish writer who emphasized the spiritual reality hidden beneath the material world. Some of the poems in *Songs of Innocence* originally appeared with a prose work *The Island in the Moon*, a satire featuring several of Blake's acquaintances thinly disguised as characters.

Songs of Innocence opens with an introductory poem in which a child encourages a piper—the lyric voice of the poem—to drop his pipe and write down his songs. Here, as in other works, Blake presents the poem's genesis with references to the physical act of putting them to paper.

"Drop the pipe thy happy pipe,
Sing thy songs of happy chear."

So I sung the same again
While he wept with joy to hear.

"Piper sit thee down and write
In a book that all may read—"
So he vanish'd from my sight.
And I pluck'd a hollow reed,

And I made a rural pen,
And I stain'd the water clear,
And I wrote my happy songs
Every child may joy to hear. (Blake 19)

This "Introduction" sets the tone for the poems that follow. Throughout the collection, innocence is represented by figures such as the child, the lamb, the shepherd, and the flower. While these figures themselves are innocent, they are not completely safe from the dangers and menaces of the world; Blake shows innocence to be a state of mind rather than a condition of the world itself. In poems such as "The Chimney Sweeper," we find that it is the children's innocence that makes them resilient enough to absorb the blows of the grim reality that surrounds them.

The figure of the lamb, which appears again and again throughout *Songs of Innocence*, has multivalent significance and thus links the various levels on which these poems can be understood. The lamb, which can represent a real lamb, a child, and Jesus, the Lamb of God or *Agnus Dei*, links the poems thematically, beginning in the "Introduction" where the child asks the piper to "Pipe a song about a Lamb" (Blake 19). Literal and figurative lambs appear throughout the collection, in "The Shepherd," "The Lamb," "The Little Black Boy," "Night," "Holy Thursday," and "Spring."   As we shall soon see, the lamb also becomes a figure of contrast with the tiger who appears in *Songs of Experience*.

Songs of Experience, first published in 1794 and issued with *Songs of Innocence* with the subtitle *Shewing the Two Contrary Sides of the Human Soul*, provides a contrast to the poems of the first volume. *Songs of Experience* opens with a poem introducing the Bard, "Who Present, Past, & Future sees" (Blake 40). This Bard appears to be the lyric voice in many of the poems, reappearing, for example, in "The Little Girl Lost," who proclaims "In futurity/ I prophetic see" (43); however, as is evident in the second poem, "Earth's Answer," the collection as a whole contains multiple voices that exist in dialogue with one another.

While the poems in *Songs of Innocence* depict an open, joyful approach to life, those in *Songs of Experience* emit a sense of self-absorbed melancholy. In *Songs of Experience*, the poet sees the corrupt world of experience, full of unhappiness, hypocrisy, evil, illness, and neglect. A number of the poems, such as "Nurses Song," "The Chimney Sweeper," and "Holy Thursday" are meant to correlate directly with poems in *Songs of Innocence*; together, these pairs of poems reveal that innocence and experience are states of mind or perspectives from which individuals may pass back and forth.

Perhaps this correlation is best illustrated by the juxtaposition of "The Tyger," Blake's best known and most anthologized poem, which appears in *Songs of Experience*, with "The Lamb" in *Songs of Innocence*. In "The Lamb," the poem begins as a series of questions address to the lamb concerning its creator:

> Little Lamb who made thee?
> Dost thou know who made thee?
> Gave thee life & bid thee feed
> By the stream & o'er the mead;
> Gave thee clothing of delight,
>
> Softest clothing wooly bright;
> Gave thee such a tender voice,
> Making all the vales rejoice:
> Little Lamb who made thee?
> Dost thou know who made thee?
>
> Little Lamb I'll tell thee,
> Little Lamb I'll tell thee:
> He is called by thy name,
> For he calls himself a Lamb:
> He is meek & he is mild,
> He became a little child:
> I a child & thou a lamb,
> We are called by his name.

Little Lamb God bless thee.
Little Lamb God bless thee.
(Blake 21–22)

The question in "The Lamb"—"Little Lamb who made thee?"—is answered by the end of the poem and followed with a blessing. Although "The Tyger" is also structured around a series of questions, there is a stark contrast in tone between the two poems. In "The Tyger," the series of rhetorical questions recalls God's questioning of Job in the Book of Job:

Tyger, Tyger, burning bright,
In the forests of the night:
What immortal hand or eye,
Could frame thy fearful symmetry?

In what distant deeps or skies
Burnt the fire of thine eyes?
On what wings dare he aspire?
What the hand dare sieze the fire?

And what shoulder, & what art,
Could twist the sinews of thy heart?
And when thy heart began to beat,
What dread hand? & what dread feet?

What the hammer? what the chain?
In what furnace was thy brain?
What the anvil? what dread grasp,
Dare its deadly terrors clasp?

When the stars threw down their spears
And water'd heaven with their tears:
Did he smile his work to see?
Did he who made the Lamb make thee?

Tyger, Tyger, burning bright,
In the forests of the night:
What immortal hand or eye,

Dare frame thy fearful symmetry?
(Blake 49–50)

While the voice addressing the "little lamb" is filled with tenderness and speaks as though to a child, the voice addressing the tiger stands back at a distance in awe. Although the lyric voice in each poem inquires into the identity of the creator, it establishes a contrast between the tiger with its "deadly terrors" (50) and the lamb, who recalls the meekness and mildness of Jesus (22). This contrast is generally interpreted as an attempt to reconcile the existence of good and evil within the same universe created by the same God (a key idea in gnosticism); hence the question posed in "The Tyger": "Did he who made the Lamb make thee?" Rather than ending with a sense of resolution and a blessing, "The Tyger" ends with "symmetry," repeating the first stanza in the final lines, as though the speaker stands frozen in awe before the vision of the tiger.

Parallels abound between the two books of songs. Images of wholesome nature that appear in *Songs of Innocence* are replaced in *Songs of Experience* with images of illness, danger, and decay, such as the beasts in "The Little Girl Lost" and "The Little Girl Found," or the invisible worm and moribund flower in "The Sick Rose." The adult as caretaker, seen in the figures of the Shepherd and the Nurse in *Songs of Innocence*, is replaced by the corrupt or negligent adult in *Songs of Experience*. In the end, these two contrasting visions of reality stand side by side without resolution.

One of the most well-known and widely discussed poems from *Songs of Experience* is "London," in which the lyric voice attests to the degradation and sorrow of modern urban life:

I wander thro' each charter'd street,
Near where the charter'd Thames does flow.
And mark in every face I meet
Marks of weakness, marks of woe.

In every cry of every Man,
In every Infant's cry of fear,
In every voice, in every ban,
The mind-forg'd manacles I hear:

How the Chimney-sweeper's cry
Every blackning Church appalls,
And the hapless Soldier's sigh,
Runs in blood down Palace walls.

But most thro' midnight streets I hear
How the youthful Harlot's curse
Blasts the new-born Infant's tear
And blights with plagues the Marriage hearse. (53)

This poem, with its mention of "mind-forg'd manacles," expresses Blake's view of man imprisoned in a hellish world of his own making. This degradation pervades society, spreading through it like a disease and affecting humankind at every stage in the cycle of life and at every level of society, from the Infant to the young Chimney-sweeper to the Soldier. The final, paradoxical image of the "Marriage hearse" attests to Blake's poetic powers, his ability to suggest a powerful, complex idea within a single phrase. "London" is particularly important in Blake's work because it clearly shows his engagement with social issues and dispels the notion that Blake was solely concerned with mystical ideas.

Together, *Songs of Innocence and Experience* became the only publication that won Blake the attention and admiration of contemporary writers like Wordsworth and Coleridge (Blake 15). The combination of simplicity and symbolism in this collection results in multiple levels of meaning that can be appreciated by adults and children alike.

MYTHOLOGY AND MORALITY

While in his earlier work these pairs of opposites are represented by stock figures and themes, in his later poetry Blake develops an entire mythology around such figures and dramatizes their struggles. These works are quite a contrast to the clarity and accessibility of *Songs of Innocence and Experience* and other earlier works. *The Book of Thel*, published in 1789, again shows the conflict between innocence and experience. The poem presents the lamentations of a young woman named Thel who avoids life because of her fear. Thel converses with lily, a cloud, and a clod of clay, each of whom reply to her lamentations—on how to live life in such a difficult environment. At the end of the poem, confronted with the dangers and uncertainties of the real world, Thel retreats from the world.

The plight of women is also the focus of *Visions of the Daughters of Albion*, published in 1793, in which Blake critiques contemporary social values regarding the treatment of women. This work was influenced in part by Blake's acquaintance with Mary Wollstonecraft, author of *A Vindication of the Rights of Women* (1792). The main character, Oothoon, is accompanied by a chorus made up of the Daughters of Albion, who bear witness to her plight; the name Albion comes from British myth of a giant who conquered the British Isles and became the forefather of the British people. Early in the poem, Oothoon, who is engaged to Theotormon, is raped by Bromion, and the remainder of the poem details the consequences of this crime as Oothoon is mistreated by Bromion and rejected by Theotormon. The mythological figure Urizen, a rigid patriarchal figure who plays an important role throughout Blake's prophetic works, first appears in *Visions*, which critiques the cruelties imposed upon women by an injust, patriarchal morality

Blake further explores issues of morality in *The Marriage of Heaven and Hell* (1790), a satirical work that challenges and plays with overturning an ossified conventional morality that enforces stark definitions of good and evil. In *Marriage*, Blake portrays a world-turned-upside-down in an attack on the philosophical trends and the religious institutions of his time. Unique in structure, *Marriage* defies generic classification; it is made up of two sets of seven parts alternating between aphoristic philosophical declarations and "Memorable Fancies"; the work ends with "The Song of Liberty," which Blake added later and which contains political allusions to the French Revolution.

In *Marriage*, Blake appears to present his Devils far more sympathetically than his Angels, leading some readers to believe that in fact the Devils are Blake's protagonists (Blake 81). Anticipating Nietzsche's *Beyond Good and Evil*, the work critiques any oversimplification of the opposition between good and evil (81), as well as the corruption of Jesus's ideals by the Church leadership. *Marriage* also turns a critical and parodic eye to the work of Swedenborg, who had influenced Blake's earlier works. Blake had by this time become more attuned to Swedenborg's conservative attitudes; *Marriage* parodies Swedenborg's *Treatise Concerning Heaven and Hell* (1784), and Blake's

"Memorable Fancies" are clearly a play on Swedenborg's "Memorable Relations" (82).

In one passage in *Marriage*, Blake calls attention to the creative labor—both physical and mental—that has gone into creating his work. This labor and the "clearing away" of "rubbish" refer both to the physical process of relief etching and to the intellectual and spiritual work of erasing ossified ideas:

> I was in a Printing house in Hell & saw the method in which knowledge is transmitted from generation to generation.
>
> In the first chamber was a Dragon-Man, clearing away the rubbish from the cave's mouth; within, a number of Dragons were hollowing the cave.
>
> In the second chamber was a Viper folding round the rock & the cave, and others adorning it with gold, silver, and precious stones.
>
> In the third chamber was an Eagle with wings and feathers of air; he caused the inside of the cave to be infinite. Around were numbers of Eagle-like men, who built palaces in the immense cliffs.
>
> In the fourth chamber were Lions of flaming fire raging around & melting the metals into living fluids.
>
> In the fifth chamber were Unnam'd forms, which cast the metals into the expanse.
>
> There they were reciev'd by Men who occupied the sixth chamber, and took the forms of books & were arranged in libraries. (Blake 94)

As in the "Introduction" to *Songs of Innocence*, Blake calls our attention here to the physical process that has gone into creating his work, reminding us again that Blake is both poet and printer, and that Blake's visionary work necessarily involved both body and soul.

THE PROPHETIC WORKS

Blake's assertion of a personal mythology is probably his most radical and revolutionary poetic act, elevating the role of the artist to something equivalent to a Biblical prophet. Blake gradually developed a personal pantheon of mythological characters meant to represent states of mind or psychological forces. These characters reappear throughout his work, taking on different roles in different narratives that attempt to dramatize the internal human condition. The main characters include Urizen, the oppressive god of reason (hence his name, which is perhaps meant as a pun on "your reason"); Orc, the rebellious spirit oppressed by Urizen; and Los, the poet-prophet who works to heal the rift within man. Many of Blake's characters split into feminine emanations, further complicating any attempt to understand Blake's mythology. While these prophetic works are at times difficult to follow, they serve to illustrate the struggle between contrary forces which forms the core theme of all of Blake's work.

In the 1790s, Blake wrote two "prophetic" works in response to the political upheavals taking place on both sides of the Atlantic. These works are prophetic not so much in terms of predicting the future, but rather in terms of interpreting and broadcasting the present political situation. In *America: A Prophecy*, dated 1793, Blake responds to the politics of the time, particularly the revolutions in America and in France. While historical references—to events such as the Boston Massacre and historical figures such as Washington—are frequent, the narrative is dramatized by the conflict between two character's from Blake's personal mythology: Orc and Urizen. *America* frames recent historical events within Blake's own mythological order, where the rebellious or revolutionary impulse takes form in the figure of Orc, who must break free from the bonds of oppression and repression imposed by his arch-enemy Urizen. Orc's struggles represent those both of the individual psyche and of the politically repressed.

Europe: A Prophecy (1794), originally intended as a sequel to *America* (Lincoln 212), rewrites the French Revolution in much the same way that *America* reworked the American Revolution, although in *Europe* no true revolution takes place. In this story, Orc's mother, Enitharmon, reigns over Europe, stifling the revolutionary impulse represented by Orc. Orc's rebellious energy is harnessed and channeled by Enitharmon and Los, who represent institutionalized Christianity. Enitharmon promulgates materialism (based on the philosophy of Francis Bacon) and the doctrine that sex is sinful. *America* and *Europe* were followed in 1795 by *The Song of Los*, which focuses in much the same way on Africa and Asia.

The First Book of Urizen, known as one of Blake's "Lambeth" works, presents Blake's somewhat comic revision of the Book of Genesis. Urizen personifies reason and patriarchal religion; he individuates himself from Los, who represents the imagination, and from the rest of the Eternals. Having split himself from the others, Urizen then attempts to impose a system of laws upon the cosmos. The Eternals reject his attempts, and Urizen must limit his creative energy to the material world he can control. Pitying Urizen, Los splits into two, and part of him becomes his feminine emanation, Enitharmon. Together, Los and Enitharmon beget Orc, who in his rage will rebel against Urizen's attempts at tyrannic control. Urizen reawakens and begets four sons, each of whom represent one of the elements: Thiriel (air), Utha (water), Grodna (earth), and Fuzon (fire). Urizen populates the earth with his progeny but then curses them to lead a frightful existence of enslavement in the material world. Fuzon later leads the surviving children of Urizen out of Egypt in Blake's version of Exodus. *The Book of Ahania* (1795) tells the story of Urizen's female emanation, Ahania. Separated from Urizen, who has rejected her, called her sin, and cast her into darkness, Ahania laments her plight. Her story is later retold in *The Four Zoas*.

In *The Four Zoas*, originally titled *Vala*, Blake further develops his personal mythology. Blake's intent was to encompass his entire mythology into a single work, but he never finished the poem. This work, an epic cosmology and universal history of civilization, revises and supplements the mythology of Blake's earlier works. *The Four Zoas* was originally intended to be divided into nine nights, after Edward Young's *Night Thoughts*, which Blake had planned to illustrate (the project later fizzled). The Zoas of the title are the four basic elements inhabiting Albion, who represents all mankind. Each of the Zoas represents part of man's nature: Urizen represents reason; Urthona represents imagination and later transforms into Los; Luvah represents passion and desire; and Tharmas represents instinct and emotion. Each Zoa is accompanied by a female Emanation: Ahania, Enitharmon, Vala, and Enion. Blake organizes the cosmos into four levels: Eden, Beulah, Generation, and Ulro. The story parallels the entire Biblical cycle, from the originating cosmogony through the end of time. Man's Fall, depicted as the separation of the Zoas, is caused by Vala, his feminine emanation. The poem ends in the ninth night with the reunification of the Zoas and their emanations. The poem, though revised, remained unfinished at the time of Blake's death.

In *Milton*, Blake outlines how the role of the poet as prophet is handed down from one generation to another—in this case, from Milton to Blake himself. John Milton (1608–1674), author of the epic poems *Paradise Lost* and *Paradise Regained*, was one of England's greatest poets, and his influence during Blake's time was particularly strong in the religious as well as the literary culture.

In writing *Milton*, Blake wishes to respond to Milton's ideas, many of which he disputed, but also hopes to harness Milton's influence and use it to his own ends. Blake disagreed with Milton's portrayal of a cold deity and his relegation of energy to the realm of the diabolical—in other words, with Milton's privileging of reason above other faculties. In the poem, Blake has Milton acknowledge and correct the error of his ways, and subsequently pass his role as poet-prophet along to Blake.

Milton opens with the poet—Blake himself—addressing the Daughters of Beulah in a passage that once again calls attention to the physical act of creation:

> Daughters of Beulah! Muses who inspire the Poet's Song
> Record the journey of immortal Milton thro' your Realms
> Of terror & mild moony luster, in soft sexual delusions
> Of varied beauty, to delight the wanderer and repose
> His burning thirst & freezing hunger! Come into my hand
> By your mild power; descending down the Nerves of my
>   right arm
> From out the Portals of my Brain[....] (Blake 239)

At the beginning of the poem, Milton is in heaven, but is unhappy because of his estrangement from his "Sixfold Emanation," which alludes to his three wives and three daughters. Moved by "a Bard's prophetic song" (240), which tells of the struggle between Satan and Palamabron, Milton returns to Earth through Blake in order to seek unification with his emanation and to pass along the role of prophet-poet to Blake. He falls through Albion, who represents universal man, struggles with Urizen, and finally enters Blake as the spirit of the poet-prophet. At the end of the poem, in an act of self-annihilation, Milton reunites with his collective emanation, Ololon. As he does so, he articulates Blake's exaltation of the imagination:

> "[....] I come in Self-annihilation & the grandeur of
>   Inspiration!
> To cast off Rational Demonstration by Faith in the Saviour,
> To cast off the rotten rags of Memory by Inspiration,
> To cast off Bacon, Locke, & Newton from Albion's covering,
> To take off his filthy garments, & clothe him with
>   Imagination!
> To cast aside from Poetry all that is not Inspiration[....]"
> (304)

Jerusalem: The Emanation of the Giant Albion applies the transcendence experience in *Milton* to the whole of the British people. Just as Milton was estranged from Ololon, Albion (England) is estranged from Jerusalem (the true spirit of Christianity). Once again, Blake retells the story of fall and redemption by weaving together his own personal mythology, Biblical narrative, and English history.

With each of these later works, Blake shows contrary forces breaking from their essential unity, coming into conflict with one another, and reunifying in an unending cycle. Despite their difficulty and obscurity, Blake's later epic works attempt, through symbolism and personification, to illuminate and dramatize the state of discord in history and the universe and to prophesy an apocalyptic reconciliation between forces in conflict. Again, the message beyond the specifics of narratives like *Milton* and *Jerusalem* is Blake's radical assertion of his personal mythology as being on the same plane as Milton's and Biblical narratives.

CONCLUSION

Ironically, the traits that obstructed the wide dispersion of Blake's works during his own time are the very same that sustain interest in and study of his work. Synthesizing word and image, myth and history, poetry and prophecy, Blake creates a new art that defies categorization. Blake's work is a radical assertion of the power and value of the individual's imagination, which is elevated to a position above that of reason or established religion. Today, Blake is regularly anthologized as an early Romantic poets and his position in the canon seems secure. But despite his secure place in the canon, his visionary approach still seems radical and revolutionary. Both the medium and the message of Blake's works may require more effort than does the poetry of Wordsworth, Coleridge, Shelley, or Keats, but in the end the reader achieves a new vision of poetry.

NOTES

1. For a brief overview of Blake within the context of the Romantic Period, see Stewart Creehan's essay "William Blake" in *The Penguin History of Literature: The Romantic Period*, ed. David B. Pirie (New York: Penguin, 1994), pp. 117–150.

2. See *Blake's Poetry and Designs*. Mary Lynn Johnson and John E. Grant, ed. (New York: W.W. Norton, 1979), p. 15.

3. See, for example, Northrop Frye, *Fearful Symmetry*, p. 11.

4. See Frye, *Fearful Symmetry* and Erdman, *Prophet Against Empire*.

5. On the relationship between Blake's words and images, see W.J.T. Mitchell, *Blake's Composite Art* (Princeton: Princeton University Press, 1978) and Jean H. Hagstrum, *William Blake: Poet and Painter*, (Chicago: University of Chicago Press, 1964).

6. As many critics have noted, Blake's vision of the struggle of creativity and imagination against repression and oppression anticipates the theories of Nietzsche, Marx, and Freud.

7. On the political and historical context of Blake's writing, see Erdman, *Prophet Against Empire*, and Saree Makdisi, *William Blake and the Impossible History of the 1790s* (Chicago: University of Chicago Press, 2003).

WORKS CITED

Blake, William. *Blake's Poetry and Designs*. Mary Lynn Johnson and John E. Grant, ed. New York: W.W. Norton, 1979.

Eaves, Morris. *The Cambridge Companion to William Blake*. Cambridge, UK: Cambridge University Press, 2003.

Frye, Northrop. *Fearful Symmetry: A Study of William Blake*. Princeton, NJ: Princeton University Press, 1947.

————. "The Keys to the Gates." *William Blake: Modern Critical Views.* Ed. Harold Bloom. New York: Chelsea House, 1985. 43–64.

Lincoln, Andrew. *Spiritual History: A Reading of William Blake's Vala or The Four Zoas.* Oxford, UK: Clarendon Press, 1996.

ROBERT F. GLECKNER

The Structure of Blake's Poetic

Only treason to his own sense of the divine
can rob the new person of his creativity.
—LEWIS MUMFORD, *The Conduct of Life*

"What was written for children can hardly offend men."[1] Thus wrote
Swinburne in 1868 about Blake's *Songs of Innocence*, and many readers
today still subscribe to this dictum. Blake himself lent credence to it by
concluding his *Introduction* to *Songs of Innocence* with:

And I wrote my happy songs
Every child may joy to hear.

A number of editions of Blake's songs have been published especially for
the young reader, and one has little doubt that children do joy to hear
them read. But Blake's "child" is a very special child, with very special
qualities, and Blake was interested not only in the joy his visions and
poems afforded but in their elucidation. "I am happy," he writes in 1799,
"to find a Great Majority of my Fellow Mortals who can Elucidate My
Visions, & Particularly they have been Elucidated by Children...."[2] "It is
pleasant enough," then, as Swinburne wrote, "to commend and to enjoy
the palpable excellence of Blake's work; but another thing is simply and
thoroughly requisite—to understand what the workman was after."[3]

From Robert F. Gleckner's *The Piper and the Bard: A Study of William Blake*, pp. 33–51, with
the permission of Wayne State University Press. © 1959 Wayne State University Press.

What was the workman after? Happy songs and sad songs, yes—*Songs of Innocence* and *Songs of Experience*—but also a poetic description of "two contrary states of the human soul." The states are of course innocence and experience, and they have been approached, explained, and commented upon in terms of mysticism, antinomianism, occultism, neo-Platonism, psychology, sociology, and autobiography. In part, at least, all of these approaches are valid, but inevitably they come to represent some sort of system or structure imposed from without. Blake's system, on the contrary, evolved organically out of the poems themselves; and it was never a static concept. This cumulative systematizing, then, is the great problem with which we must deal: to see the *Songs* as individual poems in their own right, but also to see them as integral parts of a complete book (*Songs of Innocence and of Experience*) and contributions to the formulation of a system upon which their *full* meaning largely depends.

Swinburne cautioned the readers of Blake to heed this organic unity: "They will blunder helplessly if they once fail to connect this present minute of his work with the past and future of it: if they once let slip the thinnest thread of analogy, the whole prophetic or evangelic web collapses for them into a chaos of gossamer...."[4] The explicatory chapters of this study are intended to unravel many of those analogical threads. One final problem: during the course of my analyses there will inevitably appear references to elements of Blake's system which cannot then be elucidated without undue awkwardness; further, Blake's symbols are so diverse and multivalent, his interlocking images so intricate, that occasionally one cannot see the system for the images. For these reasons, as well as to provide a general introduction to Blake's main ideas, I should like to telescope the main elements of the system, as I see them, into a bald statement of their interrelationships.

The basic conceptions of his system are ancient and elemental:[5] a supramundane and eternal world is assumed, and a fall and return are presupposed. The physical world resulted from the interaction of two elemental forces, one active and formative, the other passive and receptive; and these forces were often thought of as masculine and feminine, inner and outer. On these more or less commonplace suppositions Blake superimposed the idea that the imagination was a summation of all the members of the active, masculine series. Opposed to it he placed reason and selfhood.

In the beginning, then, before the universe appeared, was the Word or the Eternal Mind;[6]

> Earth was not: nor globes of attraction;
> The will of the Immortal expanded
> Or contracted his all flexible senses;
> Death was not, but eternal life sprung.
>
> (*Urizen*, 223)

In this primordial essence the substance of all things was contained, and from it by division and evolution each separate identity or being came into existence. Christ is that essence; all the "Eternals" "in him & he in them / Live in Perfect harmony, in Eden the land of life."[7] One of the "Eternals" is Albion, similar in conception to Swedenborg's "Grand Man, who is heaven" and the Cabbalistic Adam Kadmon. He is the symbol of all mankind as well as the universe, which has the organic unity of a man. In Eden, the eternal realm, Christ and Albion are identical for all practical purposes; their separateness is only a matter of point of view:

> Then those in Great Eternity met in the Council of God
> As one Man, for contracting their Exalted Senses
> They behold Multitude, or Expanding they behold as one,
> As One Man all the Universal family....
>
> (*Zoas*, 277)

Only as a result of a fall does the materiality of Albion constitute a distinguishable entity. Of this fall Blake will

>   Sing,
> His fall into Division & his Resurrection to Unity:
> His fall into the Generation of decay & death, & his
> Regeneration by the Resurrection from the dead.
>
> (*Zoas*, 264)

This then is Blake's starting point, a unity from which all creation emanates in some way and to which all creation strives, or should strive, to return.

Albion, the "human form divine," or Man, "anciently contain'd in his mighty limbs all things in Heaven & Earth."[8] His oneness is destroyed when, like the Gnostic man, he descends into and becomes the world of matter; but, like the Gnostic man, he collects up "the scatter'd portions of his immortal body / Into the Elemental forms of every thing that grows" and reascends (*Zoas*, 355). Significantly Albion is the human form divine as opposed to the sexual or the human form human, as I have chosen to call it: "The Sexual is Threefold: the Human is Fourfold," wrote Blake.[9] "Humanity is far above / Sexual organization" (*Jerusalem*, 721); humanity and all life are one:

> Each grain of Sand,
> Every Stone on the Land,
> Each rock & each hill,
> Each fountain & rill,
> Each herb & each tree,
> Mountain, hill, earth & sea,
> Cloud, Meteor & Star,
> Are Men Seen Afar.[10]

Since this Grand Man is endowed, then, with potential Being, he might be called more correctly the Grand Family or the Eternal Family, united as one man by common participation in eternal life.[11] Eternity is sundered when one of the eternal family usurps for himself the role of eternal man:

> If Gods combine against Man, setting their dominion above
> The Human form Divine, Thrown down from their high
>   station
> In the Eternal heavens of Human Imagination, buried beneath
> In dark Oblivion, with incessant pangs, ages on ages,
> In enmity & war first weaken'd, then in stern repentance
> They must renew their brightness, & their disorganiz'd
>   functions
> Again reorganize, till they resume the image of the human....
>   (*Zoas*, 366)

The fundamental usurpation in Blake's cosmos is that of Urizen, the rational element. His act is an act of will, which "is always Evil."[12] With this assertion of individuality, and hence of personal omniscience and omnipotence, Urizen created the world:

So he began to form of gold, silver & iron
And brass, vast instruments to measure out the immense & fix
The whole into another world better suited to obey
His will, where none should dare oppose his will, himself
    being King
Of All, & all futurity be bound in his vast chain.
(Zoas, 317)

This is the natural world of generation, strife, and death, from which
Urizen himself soon cringes and finally flees. Yet the division is not thus
limited: Urizen's self, like the human form divine from which he came,
divides against himself and produces the female emanation. The
ultimate result of this act is the war of the sexes:

When the Individual appropriates Universality
He divides into Male & Female, & when the Male & Female
Appropriate Individuality they become an Eternal Death.
(Jerusalem, 737)

Thus the active power is set into motion by two contrary forces, male
and female, positive and negative, physical and spiritual; and this power
transfers the cosmos from the plane of eternal ideal (Eternal Mind, Man,
Family) to that of finite manifestation, from the noumenal to the
phenomenal.

The theme of sex is prominent here of course. In the occult
tradition, as Denis Saurat has pointed out, "The Demiurge creates the
world or becomes the world by an act which, more or less vaguely ... is a
cosmic parallel to the sexual act. In its extreme expression we find the
hermaphrodite God, who divides himself and whose parts fecundate each
other."[13] Blake posits sexual union as the one valid method of reachieving
the eternal oneness. Of the two separated halves of our sexually divided
self woman, the emanative passive contrary, is restrained. Even though she
is the emotional element in life, once separated from the rational or
intellectual element, she is afraid of passion; she is chaste, jealous, and
intolerant, given to secrecy and guile. Most of the women in *Songs of
Experience* embody these traits. The active contrary, man or spectre, is
intellectually uncertain instead of aggressive, fearful and inhibited instead
of experimental. Theotormon in *Visions of the Daughters of Albion* is a good

example of this. In his impotence the male contrary is, like Arthur, "Woman-born / And Woman-nourish'd & Woman-educated & Woman-scorn'd!" (*Jerusalem*, 698). An effort of will cannot unite Urizen again with the human form divine; only a denial of self and the concomitant selfless, creative union with his emanation can accomplish this.

Separated from the divine One, Urizen becomes Reason incarnate, the emanations become feeling or emotion, and each desires the other but tries to conquer rather than yield to the other's dominion. On the human level this takes the form of sexual strife, and it is always severance from spiritual life which precedes the separation of emanation from body. "Rent from Eternal Brotherhood we die & are no more" (*Zoas*, 293). Only when spiritual life is regained can reunion take place. So long as there is separation, the struggle for predominance goes on, the dependent part or emanation developing for the purposes of contention a will of its own, the "female will." "In Eternity Woman is the Emanation of Man; she has No Will of her own. There is no such thing in Eternity as a Female Will" (*Last Judgment*, 613). The reunion, therefore, can only be consummated by an imaginative act, a creation, which involves at once the denial of reason and emotion individually and the acceptance of both. Without the requisite denials there is only the repetitive rape of Oothoon by Bromion (*Visions of the Daughters of Albion*), each a reassertion of the fact of division.

The world created by this division is, as I have said, one of generation, strife, and death. Urizen—or popularly Jehovah—institutes the iron-clad law to rule his subjects, to keep them in a state of subservience to himself:

> Lo! I unfold my darkness, and on
> This rock place with strong hand the Book
> Of eternal brass, written in my solitude:
> Laws of peace, of love, of unity,
> Of pity, compassion, forgiveness;
> Let each curse one habitation,
> His ancient infinite mansion,
> One command, one joy, one desire,
> One curse, one weight, one measure,
> One King, one God, one Law.
>   (*Urizen*, 224)

The cleverness of Urizen's propagandistic approach is worth noting: the appeal of the virtues, and their complete submergence under one law, Urizen's. But such a bearing of indisputable rule brings with it continual revolt and further restraint—the laws of society, morality, religion, science, marriage, the laws which strangle the human and perpetuate the original fall into ultimate non-entity, the depths of division. In effect Urizen loses control of the creation because of the very method of control which he has imposed upon it.

At this point the creation is assumed by the hand of the human form divine. A limit is placed on the fall to prevent utter annihilation and a reversion to chaos, Boehme's "eternal Abyss."

> Thus were the stars of heaven created like a golden chain
> To bind the Body of Man to heaven from falling into the Abyss.
> (*Zoas*, 287)

The limit is Adam, the natural world. "Creation," said Blake, "was an act of Mercy" (*Last Judgment*, 614).

> For the Divine Lamb, Even Jesus who is the Divine Vision,
> Permitted all, lest Man should fall into Eternal Death.
> (*Zoas*, 287)

Thus, while the fall was originally Urizen's responsibility, dictated by a rational act of will, the creation of man himself was the province of the divine imagination; man was created so that he could rise from the fall, overcome blind reason, and reachieve the imaginative realm. With the arrest of the retrogressive effect of the fall by the formation of man's corporeal, mortal body, which Blake calls the "limit of contraction," man becomes bound to the realm of time and space. Nevertheless, though fallen through Urizen's revolt, he is still a spark of the divine: "Human nature is the image of God"; "God is a man."[14] But caverned in his body of five senses, man fails to perceive that the reality underlying everything is a portion of eternity and therefore infinite:

> The Visions of Eternity, by reason of narrowed perceptions,

Are become weak Visions of Time & Space, fix'd into
furrows of death.

(Jerusalem, 679)

"The roaring of lions, the howling of wolves, the raging of the stormy
sea. and the destructive sword. are portions of eternity too great for the
eye of man."[15] To regain the ability to perceive eternity is prerequisite
to reunion or, popularly, salvation.

2

That in briefest outline is Blake's cosmic system. To relate it to the
world of the *Songs of Innocence and of Experience* we must restate the
outline in several different terms, the progression of those terms leading
us from the cosmic plane eventually to the plane of child, man, woman
in the states of innocence and experience. To return to the primal unity,
then, the Eternal Family which makes up the Eternal Man is composed
of what might be called unconscious selves, all parts of a greater, all-
embracing self, the human form divine. In these terms Urizen's revolt is
a separation of the individual self from the divine selfhood, the latter
being a positive good, the former, evil in the sense that it is intrinsically
negative.[16] Thus individualized, Urizen's self arranges and governs the
world as if he were the human form divine and everything were a part of
him. The creation is for his profit, and to his self accrues all its benefits.
In this situation the way to reunion lies in recognizing the existence of
one's selfhood and then denying it by merging with another self, the
emanation. Or, as Blake put it in *A Vision of the Last Judgment*,
"Whenever any Individual Rejects Error & Embraces Truth, a Last
Judgment passes upon that Individual" (613). Or again, in terms Blake
establishes in *The Marriage of Heaven and Hell* (155), whereas selfhood is
all-devouring, the denial of self is prolific. The union (not the
reconciliation) of self with self, on selfless terms, can then reinstitute the
condition of unconscious selfhood which preceded Urizen's revolt.

This cosmic myth, however, also includes the fall and rise of the
imagination. Again, to paraphrase St. John, "In the beginning was the
Eternal Mind." It alone is real. It is also "the most Prolific of All Things
& Inexhaustible" and hence is identified with "Imagination, which is
Spiritual Sensation" or the "Spiritual Perception" Sir Joshua Reynolds

was so anxious to disprove.[17] This spiritual perception constitutes the Divine Vision of "what Eternally Exists, Really & Unchangeably."[18] In fact, Imagination is eternity. Within this dialectic the fall is a process of contraction in which the clarity of imaginative vision is obscured by ratiocination. With each successive division from the primal unity of imagination or the human form divine, eternal or fourfold vision becomes darker and darker, and man, though still a portion of the eternal, is enclosed more tightly in the prison of the five senses "till he sees all things thro' narrow chinks of his cavern" (*Marriage*, 154). His "senses unexpansive in one stedfast bulk remain" and cannot penetrate beyond the bounds of self, "As the tree knows not what is outside of its leaves and bark" (*Zoas*, 305, 314). This is what Blake called single vision, the limit of opacity, Ulro, complete darkness. "Natural objects always ... weaken, deaden & obliterate Imagination," he said; "The Natural Body is an Obstruction to the Soul or Spiritual Body." "I assert for My Self that I do not behold the outward Creation & that to me is a hindrance & not Action; it is as the Dirt upon my feet, No part of Me."[19] The dichotomy between the natural man and the imaginative man is made most clear in Blake's tractate, *There Is No Natural Religion*, etched before the *Songs of Innocence*:

> *The Argument.* Man has no notion of moral fitness but from Education. Naturally he is only a natural organ subject to Sense.
>
> I. Man cannot naturally Percieve but through his natural or bodily organs.
>
> II. Man by his reasoning power can only compare & judge of what he has already perciev'd.
>
> III. From a perception of only 3 senses or 3 elements none could deduce a fourth or fifth.
>
> IV. None could have other than natural or organic thoughts if he had none but organic perceptions.
>
> V. Man's desires are limited by his perceptions, none can desire what he has not perciev'd.
>
> VI. The desires & perceptions of man, untaught by any thing but organs of sense, must be limited to objects of sense.
>
> *Conclusion*: If it were not for the Poetic or Prophetic character the Philosophic & Experimental would soon be at

the ratio of all things, & stand still, unable to do other than repeat the same dull round over again.

This is Ulro and Generation. The return from these lower depths to imaginative vision is hinted at in the "Second Series" of this same tractate:

> I. Man's perceptions are not bounded by organs of perception; he percieves more than sense (tho' ever so acute) can discover.
> II. Reason, or the ratio of all we have already known, is not the same that it shall be when we know more.
> III. [This proposition is lost.]
> IV. The bounded is loathed by its possessor. The same dull round, even of a universe, would soon become a mill with complicated wheels.
> V. If the many become the same as the few when possess'd, Morel Morel is the cry of a mistaken soul; less than All cannot satisfy Man.
> VI. If any could desire what he is incapable of possessing, despair must be his eternal lot.
> VII. The desire of Man being Infinite, the possession is Infinite & himself Infinite.
> *Application.* He who sees the Infinite in all things, sees God.
> He who sees the Ratio only, sees himself only.
> Therefore God becomes as we are, that we may be as he is.

But with the fallen imagination contracted into the five senses, how does one ever see the infinite in all things? Blake answers the question in *The Marriage of Heaven and Hell*: "This will come to pass by an improvement of sensual enjoyment" (154), that is, through the imagination who is Jesus Christ, the Saviour. "Therefore God becomes as we are, that we may be as he is." This is the key to all of Blake's poetry. In this concept of salvation the rise from division, the denial of self, the reachievement of imaginative vision, and the descent and resurrection of Christ are all merged.

The first step toward such salvation is the recognition of self as the great evil, as error incarnate, and the consequent denial of it for a place in the greater self. "One Error not remov'd will destroy a human Soul" (*Jerusalem*, 676); "to be an Error & to be Cast out is a part of God's design" (*Last Judgment*, 613). Parallel to this denial or casting out is the realization that a rational approach to life gives only a ratio rather than the whole picture; man's vision, instead of being directed outward, is turned in upon itself by the walls of the five senses and he "sees himself only."[20] Hence, Blake's insistence upon an *improvement* of sensual enjoyment. This does not mean, as many have believed, free love or anything of the sort, but rather a breaking of the mundane shell of the five senses, a conscious violation of the moral, religious, and social law which exists for its own or Urizen's sake, and which stifles energy and life at every turn. Promiscuity is not the answer, but neither is chastity. This is one of the points on which Blake and Swedenborg very nearly agree. For the former, chastity was anathema since it presupposed a restrictive law, not necessarily ethical, but restrictive to action; the latter believed more or less the same thing although he stated it in somewhat different terms. Still those terms do express more clearly than any of Blake's prose approximately what he meant by ideal sexual union:

> ... Love truly conjugial is chastity itself. The reasons are these: (1) Because it is from the Lord, and corresponds to the marriage of the Lord and the church. (2) Because it descends from the marriage of good and truth. (3) Because it is spiritual, just in the degree that the church is with man. (4) Because it is the fundamental love, and the head of all loves, celestial and spiritual. (5) Because it is the true seminary of the human race, and thence of the angelic heaven. (6) Because it therefore exists also among the angels of heaven, and with them spiritual offspring are born of it, which are love and wisdom. (7) And because its use is thus pre-eminent above all the other uses of creation. From this it follows that love truly conjugial, viewed from its origin and in its essence, is pure and holy, so that it may be called purity and holiness, and therefore chastity itself.[21]

For Blake, however, action, not the bond of marriage, was the one solution, for all act is good and virtuous and all prohibition of action, whether in others or in the self, is evil or vicious.

In other words, life must be positive according to Blake, and this is impossible as long as any kind of restraint invokes an everlasting nay. To act in terms of the self alone is to prevent action on the part of another; to act according to reason is to limit sensual enjoyment; to act for one's own good according to one's own individual preference is to isolate the self completely from the all-inclusive self of the human form divine. Hence Blake's equation of reunion, revivification of imaginative vision, and Christ's sacrifice. He became as we are—that is he denied his self to *produce* action in men; once on earth he acted not from the rules but from impulse[22] so that his life was the epitome of improved sensual enjoyment. And he acted for the good of all to reorganize the human form divine.[23] This is the main reason, of course, why Blake can unite the imagination, the poetic or prophetic character, and man himself all in the person of Jesus Christ. He is the human form *divine* just as man, fallen, is the human form *human*, and man, reunited in the Eternal Man or Family, is the human form *divine*.

Blake's use of Christ's relationship to Mary is also pertinent here, especially in view of the doctrine of the virgin birth. A chaste ethics, of course, was synonymous in Blake's mind with the moral law, natural religion; and yet "Christ's very being," as Milton O. Percival says, "is a repudiation of the religion which engendered him." Mary stands at once "for the chastity of a restrictive ethics and, by having given birth to an illegitimate child, for a forgiveness which defies chastity."[24] She represents the law and freedom from the law. As the former, she is that humanity which Christ must put off eternally "Lest the Sexual Generation swallow up Regeneration" (*Jerusalem*, 737). Out of the cruelty of dark religions, just as out of experience, come the forgiveness of sins and the higher innocence.

The recreative union of the separate selves has a corollary in imaginative creation, as that act applies to man's attempt to reachieve eternity. As we have seen, the division into male and female was a direct result of the initial cosmic fall. Reuniting these two contraries demands the greatest of human acts, sexual union. "In Eternity the lover and loved are literally one," said St. Matthew. But it is a very special kind of sexual union of which Blake wrote, one which involves his concepts of prolific and devourer, spectre and emanation. The mere reconciliation of the two is not the solution; indeed Blake believed that earthly "Religion is an endeavour to reconcile the two" and "whoever tries to reconcile them seeks to destroy existence." "Without Contraries is no progression" (*Marriage*, 155, 149). To join the two and yet maintain their respective "contrariety," Blake introduced the idea of creation as opposed to mere copulation, Swedenborg's scortatory love; the latter, however defined, is not what Blake meant by an improvement of sensual enjoyment. It is lust, a debasement of sensual enjoyment. The male must at once give and take to satisfy Blake's conditions, and the female must at once take and give. The former gives of the seminal fluid in the process of creation, but at the same time he "devours" the woman's body; the woman gives herself while at the same time devouring the seed. In these terms the sexual act is tacit recognition of the eternal union and the personal participation in that union; the proof lies in the creation—in this case the child, in the poet's case a poem. In either case, the senses per se are penetrated by the light of vision and the act becomes what Blake calls a last judgment, the final reunion.

But what of the child, the creation itself? For this we must turn to Blake's conception of innocence, experience, and a higher innocence.

3

In the *Songs of Innocence* the child is the symbol of primal unity, for all practical purposes a God. He is an unconscious self; or, in other words, innocence is the Eternal Family united in God by common participation in eternal life. But it is not quite the same. Blake has lowered the frame of reference from the cosmic to the human; fourfold vision in eternity, the unified imagination, has given way here to its approximation on earth, the highest plane which mortal man can reach. Blake calls it Beulah, the realm of the sun's reflection, the realm of the moon, the realm of threefold vision. In Beulah the child is born, and for him it is a paradise on earth; for the parents it is the ultimate step (creation) before reunion with the human form divine. The characteristics of innocence are those of eternity: perfect happiness in ignorance of evil and the self; freedom and energy without restrictive law; unhindered communion between the child's life and the lives of animals and the surrounding universe; and the clear vision (which is love) of the divine world. The child revels in all of this and is protected from premature division by the earthly mother and the spiritual father, for the child is part human, part divine. The time must come, however, when the child achieves adolescence, the mind begins to develop, and the senses mature. At this point experience must be entered without the guiding hand of an earthly mother or spiritual father. Given the world of contraries, both must be experienced to achieve the ultimate union in Beulah, and finally Eternity. Those contraries we have already seen as prolific and devourer; here they are innocence and experience, unconscious selfhood and conscious selfhood.

In these human terms Blake's fall is a movement from pristine unconsciousness into self-consciousness; the child becomes aware of his separate impulses and their conflicts. The transcendence of experience (or separation) lies in reintegration and, as Schorer put it, "in the achievement of a higher consciousness that is without the strife of the middle state but is also aware as the first was not."[25] Every child is born a self, despite Swedenborg's denial of a "proprium" for him, but in innocence that self is unrecognized as such, even while it is being indulged promiscuously. As long as this ignorance obtains, the primal unity is not threatened. Yet infantilism is not what Blake was after. He envisioned an organized innocence, an "Innocence [that] dwells with Wisdom, but never with Ignorance." Childhood is the realm of ignorance. To know implies first of all self-knowledge, and self-knowledge can only be gained by realizing one's own corporeal existence in relation to the rest of the universe. It is self-identification. At this point the crisis of the child's life has been reached—to see the self as the great evil contrary in the world and to deny that contrary in favor of the over-all self which is the human form divine. As Bronowski expressed it in striking language, "The child must take and must murder experience; it must become father and hypocrite; and it will have found itself if that iron cruelty has rewritten innocence."[26] Now it should be especially clear why Blake thought of the creation—or experience—as an act of mercy: within experience and only within experience can the spark of divine light be enlarged and brightened to grow into a higher innocence. "Experience," as Percival says, "is remedial."[27] In cosmic terms the child divides itself into self and self-less, into the reasoning spectre and the affectionate emanation. The two must be rejoined in an imaginative creation like that which unites prolific and devourer.

In experience of course this is particularly difficult because there all freedom, energy, desire, and vision are throttled by the man-made law of father, priest, and king. These three, a composite Urizen, must be conquered. Collectively they are experience, and they produce the harlot (Blake's "virgin"), religion, morality, and jealousy. Yet they are not the real enemy, for they are basically symbolic manifestations of the perversities of all human nature. The real enemy is the individual self, through which father, priest, and king can reach the individual soul, and it is the self which must be recognized as experience and ultimately denied. The ministering mother of the state of innocence is no longer there for protection—indeed, if she is there she is a tyrant; but the father is there and he is a Urizen or a Tiriel. The only way to overcome him is by an improvement of sensual enjoyment, by thwarting law, by cleansing the windows of perception, and by achieving a vision of the eternal unity that can be achieved only through selfless creation. This is the state Swedenborg described as "The innocence of wisdom ... genuine innocence ... it is eternal: for it belongs to the mind itself."[28] Precisely how Blake meant this state to be reached lies within the province of the prophetic books and hence not within the limits of this discussion. The present state of the soul was the subject of the *Songs*.

4

In the progression from childhood to maturity and marriage, from innocence to experience to a higher innocence in wisdom, there are two main ideas which predominate, joy and love. They are by no means mutually exclusive ideas and they are not strictly definable; yet, their interdependence provides the reader with the key to what Blake meant when he wrote, "Generation, Image of regeneration" (*Jerusalem*, 626). At the core of his system, they encompass Christ and the child, the father and mother, imagination and vision.

The happiness of the child in innocence is by nature selfish and instinctive, although, as we have seen, that selfishness is not a conscious attitude. The child lives for itself in much the same fashion that eternity exists for itself. On the other hand, Blake wrote, "Eternity is in love with the productions of time" (*Marriage*, 151), and "The Ruins of Time builds Mansions in Eternity" (Letter to Hayley, 797). It is with time that both innocence and experience have to do. To continue the selfish and instinctive life results in the pseudo-joy of the vales of Har and Heva, a joy predicated on the fact of the self's existing only for the self. This was Har's error in creating his race of men in *Tiriel*, the race of Tiriels which makes up this world. Actually, at maturity—or from the advent of experience on—man can experience a happiness much greater than can ever be known by the child, for it is no longer selfish and instinctive but inclusive and imaginative.

Hence the state of experience is at once a state of disillusionment and the origin of a potential guiding light for all mankind; individuation and unity go hand in hand. Blake's general symbol of experience is the grave, and the voice of the grave at the end of *The Book of Thel* is his most explicit and concise description of the state. The soul is on the horns of a dilemma: to share the joy which it has so happily and irresponsibly reveled in alone in innocence, or to keep the joy as its own and retreat with it to the vales of Har. But Blake makes unmistakably clear in *Thel* and *Tiriel* that the soul is not self-sufficient. Indeed it was not self-sufficient even in innocence, for the earthly mother helped to keep innocence inviolate, and the spiritual father was there to restate the fact of innocence at crucial moments like that in *The Little Boy Found*. Man must pass out of innocence; there is no real choice if imagination and the higher innocence are to be reached.

Vaguely similar to a "fortunate fall," the Blakean fall from innocence to experience is necessary so that each of us, through a last judgment, may live eternally. F.C. Prescott has put it in a more modern context: "Even this garden has been but a stopping-place for the human mind; however longingly we look back to it we cannot return; when we have once taken our departure the path leading toward it is fatally regressive."[29] In other words there is actually a difference between the cosmic fall and the human fall, though Blake does merge them constantly in his system. Urizen's fall was a result of willful revolt and hence an unnecessary "accident"; with the subsequent creation of humankind the fall became a necessity so that man could recognize the selfhood of error that is his legacy from Urizen. If the self persists in its ways beyond childhood and innocence, without self-consciousness, it will be unable to know the joy of brotherhood or any other kind of unity. Without imagination, which links his life with all that is beyond his life, man remains in the grave of memory,[30] stagnant from here to eternity. That stagnation was called by Blake the joyless moral law, which imposed general form upon the inherently individual human form divine. For his salvation, man ironically does not look outside himself but within, not to the self which is man's approximation of the divine, but to his essential humanity which *is* divine. Urizen was divine to begin with, but he felt he had to usurp divinity to assert that fact before the cosmic audience. "God is no more," said Blake in *The Everlasting Gospel* (756); God is Jehovah, the very "without" that imposes the iron-clad law. "Thine own Humanity learn to Adore," for "where is the Father of men to be seen but in the most perfect of his children?"[31]

> I am not a God afar off, I am a brother and friend;
>   Within your bosoms I reside, and you reside in me.
>   (*Jerusalem*, 622)

When man can see that, as the child does in *A Little Boy Lost* for example, the windows of the morning have once again been opened.

Vision, of course, precludes restraint. "Thou shalt not" is the form restraint takes in this world; instinct and passion are banned in favor of reason and abstinence. Spiritual purpose is completely denied to instinctive life by earthly morality. Thus, the purpose of experience in Blake's system is, in Max Plowman's phrase, the "imaginative redemption of instinct."[32] Then and only then will the five senses appear as inlets to the soul.

Love has much the same history as joy-instinct, for Blake saw God as love. Hence man, too, is love. In innocence love is as selfish as joy has been seen to be, both founded on ignorance. With the advent of experience, however, love must find an object. There are many, of course, but all of them ultimately come under the headings of love of another and love of self. Swedenborg, for example, divides love into two groups of two: "There are in heaven two distinct kinds of love—love to the Lord, and love towards the neighbor." The former is celestial love, the latter spiritual. "But ... Man is not born to those two Kinds of Love, but to their Contraries, viz. to Self-Love and the Love of the World...."[33] Though Blake could not agree with this idea of original sin, he did agree wholeheartedly with the basic dichotomy. To pursue the love of self even after innocence recedes into the past is to turn to the past and memory, to go the way of Thel when she fled the grave in horror. To love others is to love God. "The worship of God is. Honouring his gifts in other men each according to his genius, and loving the greatest men best, those who envy or calumniate great men hate God. for there is no other God."[34] "Thine own Humanity learn to

Adore." Love is a process of becoming one, but like the prolific and devourer, it is not complete self-abnegation. The fulfillment of two desires is necessary: the prolific is also devouring, as we have seen, and the devourer is prolific. Man cannot give himself until he possesses himself through self-assertion; imagination cannot function except through the individual who has realized himself. Similarly, love without sensual enjoyment is sterile, and sensual enjoyment, redeemed from lust by imagination, thus becomes neither selfishness nor self-denial but a marriage of the two.

So far from free love is Blake's "improvement of sensual enjoyment," then, that we may read his phrase with equal correctness as "an improvement of spiritual enjoyment." For soul and body are always one in Blake's system. When the senses are enjoyed as the true inlets of the soul through which spiritual perceptions (multifold vision) can be made, then matter can no longer hamper soul, the doors of perception will be clean, and everything will appear as it is, infinite.

5

Despite this threefold scheme I have been outlining, Blake's system actually breaks down into four steps. I insist on three here only because the fourth and lowest is seldom mentioned in connection with the songs, and indeed has very little significance, for our purposes, beyond what we would call chaos. As we have seen, Blake called it Ulro, the lowest state of the cosmos after Urizen's revolt, or single vision, which sees the self only. Above Ulro's darkness is what I have been calling experience, Blake's Generation, the realm of the flesh, this world, within which there is potentially double vision. With double vision man can see beyond the self and the mere facts of existence to recognize the human. But experience is also the world of "goodness," which "is the passive that obeys Reason" (*Marriage*, 149), and of the moral law, under which the sacredness of all life is denied and an ethics of repression superimposed on it. With the divine world hidden, the worship of God takes the form of man-made law in empty, hypocritical ceremony. Jealousy stalks the battlefield between the warring contraries, and fear is the only password. Natural religion enmeshes all life and the highest vision attainable is man. God is no more.[35]

God returns in Beulah with its threefold vision, in which the divine is visible in the human. This as we have seen is the realm of the highest union on earth, the union which approaches in all respects a final reintegration with eternity and the human form divine. Blake's choice of the name, Beulah (which means "married"), to symbolize the felicitous relationship of the two main contraries, man and woman, is thus most apt. In the ideally married state the jealousy of experience has no place, the outer and inner worlds are in harmony (Swedenborg's "equilibrium") and at peace, for no portion of life is denied. As Blake wrote in *Jerusalem*:

> Embraces are Cominglings from the Head even to the Feet,
> And not a pompous High Priest entering by a Secret Place
> (708)

as is the case in Generation, where forgiveness has been lost sight of in the mysteries of the moral law.

The final reintegration is Eden, fourfold vision, the innocence of wisdom, where all is love and all is one. Mercy, pity, peace are all included here in the Divine Man, Adam Kadmon, the Imagination. It is Blake's Heaven.

With these manifold—and shifting—patterns in mind, we can undertake a detailed analysis of each contributive element as it evolved in Blake's mind and poetry; but before that can be done we must examine Blake's method of presenting those elements.

NOTES

1. William Blake: A Critical Essay (London, 1906), p. 140.

2. Letter to Trusler in Geoffrey Keynes, *The Complete Writings of William Blake* (London, 1957), p. 794. All subsequent page references in the text to Blake's works will be to this edition, though for the major works under discussion I shall retain consistently Blake's punctuation rather than Keynes's.

3. *William Blake: A Critical Study*, p. 140.

4. *Ibid.*, p. 161.

5. There has been considerable discussion about how much of his system Blake derived from others, particularly Boehme, Swedenborg, and various neo-Platonists. The ideas of a primal unity, a fall into

division, and a return to unity are of course not new, and no one can deny that there are many isolated instances of congeniality between Blake and various philosophers, theologians, pseudo-scientists, Gnostics, Cabbalists, and so forth. In none of them, however, is there an adumbration of Blake's system as I shall define it, except insofar as many of their symbols turn up in Blake's poetry. Even here Blake's mind did with them what it would, and my occasional references to a "source" are more as an aid to clarification than a suggestion of indebtedness. That Blake's system only gradually developed, with many fits and starts, is adequate proof of its essential originality. For the controversy over the influence of other writers see especially Mark Schorer, *William Blake: The Politics of Vision* (New York, 1946), pp. 104–148; J.G. Davies, *The Theology of William Blake* (Oxford, 1948), pp. 35–49; Paul Berger, *William Blake: Poet and Mystic*, trans. Danid H. Connor (New York, 1915), pp. 13, 55, 57, 198–208, 211–220; Helen C. White, *The Mysticism of William Blake* (Madison, 1927), pp. 128–164; David V. Erdman, *William Blake: Prophet against Empire* (Princeton, 1956), *passim*; and a group of scattered articles and essays by George Mills Harper and Kathleen Raine.

6. Blake never uses the former term in this sense, but for his use of the latter see *The First Book of Urizen*, 227 (hereafter referred to as *Urizen*).

7. *The Four Zoas*, 277, hereafter referred to as *Zoas*.

8. "To the Jews," *Jerusalem*, 649.

9. *Milton*, 483. Cf. *Zoas*, 264:
Four Mighty Ones are in every Man; a Perfect Unity
Cannot Exist but from the Universal Brotherhood of Eden,
The Universal Man....

10. Letter to Butts, 805. Cf. *A Vision of the Last Judgment*, 605-606, and especially the Annotations to Lavater's *Aphorisms*, 87.

11. See, e.g., *Zoas*, 374; *Jerusalem*, 664–665.

12. Annotations to Swedenborg, 89.

13. *Literature and the Occult Tradition*, trans. Dorothy Bolton (London, 1930), pp. 17–18.

14. Annotations to Lavater, 83; Annotations to Swedenborg, 90.

15. *The Marriage of Heaven and Hell*, 151, hereafter cited as *Marriage*.

16. See Blake's Annotations to Lavater, 77 (no. 409) and 88 (no. 640). See also *Last Judgment*, 615, par. 2.

17. Annotations to Reynolds, 471; Letter to Trusler, 794; Annotations to Reynolds, 473.

18. *Last Judgment*, 604. In this work is a good example of what Blake probably meant by "spiritual sensation." Speaking of his painting of the Last Judgment he says: "If the Spectator could Enter into these Images in his Imagination, approaching them on the Fiery Chariot of his Contemplative Thought, if he could Enter into Noah's Rainbow or into his bosom, or could make a Friend & Companion of one of these Images of wonder, which always intreats him to leave mortal things (as he must know), then would he arise from his Grave [i.e., this world], then would he meet the Lord in the Air & then he would be happy" (611). See also Chapter III of this study for an examination of Blake's technique as an application of his theory of the symbolic imagination.

19. Annotations to Wordsworths' *Poems*, 783; Annotations to Berkeley's *Siris*, 775; *Last Judgment*, 617.

20. This is what Blake scrupulously avoided in all of his work. In one place he wrote: "'What,' it will be Question'd, 'When the Sun rises, do you not see a round disk of fire somewhat like a Guinea?' 0 no, no, I see an Innumerable company of the Heavenly host crying, 'Holy, Holy, Holy is the Lord God Almighty.' I question not my Corporeal or Vegetative Eye any more than I would Question a Window concerning a Sight. I look thro' it & not with it" (*Last Judgment*, 617). Cf. *Auguries of Innocence*, 433–434, lines 125–128.

21. *The Delights of Wisdom Pertaining to Conjugial Love after which Follow The Pleasures of Insanity Pertaining to Scortatory Love* (New York, 1910), p. 157, par. 143.

22. *The Everlasting Gospel*, 748–759. See also *Marriage*, 158.

23. I use the word "reorganize" here advisedly since Blake insisted, "unorganiz'd Innocence: An Impossibility. Innocence dwells with Wisdom, but never with Ignorance" (Notes written on a page of *Zoas*, 380). Cf. *Zoas*, 366, lines 363–374.

24. *William Blake's Circle of Destiny* (New York, 1938), pp. 123–124. See Blake's *Everlasting Gospel*, 753–757.

25. *William Blake: The Politics of Vision*, p. 268.

26. *A Man without a Mask* (London, 1947), p. 135.

27. *William Blake's Circle of Destiny*, pp. 11–12.

28. *Heaven and Its Wonders, the World of Spirits, and Hell: From Things Heard and Seen*, trans. Rev. Samuel Noble (New York 1864), p. 134, par. 278.

29. *Poetry and Myth* (New York, 1927), p. 173.

30. Ellis and Yeats define this idea with admirable precision: Urizen falls "into chaos, which is memory, because memory is the record of the merely egoistic experience, thus differing from inspiration, which is direct experience."—*The Works of William Blake* (3 vols., London, 1893), I, 252.

31. *The Everlasting Gospel*, 750; statement by Lavater, underlined by Blake and called "ture worship" (82).

32. *An Introduction to the Study of Blake* (London, 1927), p. 133.

33. *Heaven and Its Wonders ... and Hell*, p. 9, par. 15; p. 13, par. 23; *Concerning the Earths in Our Solar System which Are Called Planets*, trans. anon. (London, 1787), pp. 116–117.

34. *Marriage*, 158. Swedenborg could never hold such a view as this, since he never identified the evil man with the all-good God. Indeed he probably would have reacted to this statement in the *Marriage* much as the angel did when he heard Blake's devil speak the words: "The Angel hearing this became almost blue but mastering himself he grew yellow, & at last white pink & smiling. and then replied, Thou Idolater, is not God One? & is not he visible in Jesus Christ? and has not Jesus Christ given his sanction to the law of ten commandments and are not all other men fools. sinners & nothings."

35. See, e.g., *Urizen*, 235–236; *The Book of Ahania*, 255; *Zoas*, 374; *Milton*, 517–518; *Jerusalem*, 679–680, 724–725.

NORTHROP FRYE

Blake's Introduction to Experience

Students of literature often think of Blake as the author of a number of lyrical poems of the most transparent simplicity, and of a number of "prophecies" of the most impenetrable complexity. The prophecies are the subject of some bulky commentaries, including one by the present writer, which seem to suggest that they are a special interest, and may not even be primarily a literary one. The ordinary reader is thus apt to make a sharp distinction between the lyrical poems and the prophecies, often with a hazy and quite erroneous notion in his mind that the prophecies are later than the lyrics, and represent some kind of mental breakdown.

Actually Blake, however versatile, is rigorously consistent in both his theory and practice as an artist. The *Poetical Sketches*, written mostly in his teens, contain early lyrics and early prophecies in about equal proportions. While he was working on the *Songs of Innocence and of Experience*, he was also working on their prophetic counterparts. While he was working at Felpham on his three most elaborate prophecies, he was also writing the poems in the Pickering MS, which include such pellucid lyrics as "Mary," "William Bond," and "The Smile." The extent to which the prophecies themselves are permeated by a warm and simple lyrical feeling may be appreciated by any reader who does not shy at the proper names. Hence the method, adopted in some critical studies, including my own *Fearful Symmetry*, of concentrating on the prophecies and neglecting the lyrics on the ground that they can be understood

From *Huntington Library Quartet* XXI (1957), pp. 57–67. Henry E. Huntington Library and Art Gallery.

without commentary, may have the long-run disadvantage of compromising with a thoroughly mistaken view of Blake.

What I propose to do here is to examine one of Blake's shortest and best known poems in such a way as to make it an introduction to some of the main principles of Blake's thought. The poem selected is the "Introduction" to the *Songs of Experience*, which for many reasons is as logical a place as any to begin the study of Blake. I do not claim that the way of reading it set forth here is necessary for all readers, but only that for those interested in further study of Blake it is a valid reading.

> Hear the voice of the Bard!
> Who Present, Past & Future, sees;
> Whose ears have heard
> The Holy Word
> That walk'd among the ancient trees ...

This stanza tells us a great deal about Blake's view of the place and function of the poet. The second line, repeated many years later in *Jerusalem* ("I see the Past, Present & Future existing all at once Before me"), establishes at once the principle that the imagination unifies time by making the present moment real. In our ordinary experience of time we are aware only of three unrealities: a vanished past, an unborn future, and a present that never quite comes into existence. The center of time is now, yet there never seems to be such a time as now. In the ordinary world we can bind experience together only through the memory, which Blake declares has nothing to do with imagination. There is no contact with any other points of time except those that have apparently disappeared in the past. As Proust says, in such a world our only paradises can be the paradises that we have lost. For Blake, as for Eliot in the "Quartets," there must also be another dimension of experience, a vertical timeless axis crossing the horizontal flow of time at every moment, providing in that moment a still point of a turning world, a moment neither in nor out of time, a moment that Blake in the prophecies calls the moment in each day that Satan cannot find.

The worst theological error we can make, for Blake, is the "Deist" one of putting God at the beginning of the temporal sequence, as a First Cause. Such a view leads logically to an absolute fatalism, though its devotees are seldom so logical. The only God worth worshipping is a

God who, though in his essence timeless, continually enters and redeems time, in other words an incarnate God, a God who is also Man. There is a Trinity in Blake of Father, Son, and Spirit, but Blake takes very seriously the Christian doctrines that the Spirit proceeds from the Son and that no man can know the Father except through the Son, the humanity of God. Attempts to approach the Father directly produce what Blake calls "Nobodaddy," whom we shall meet again in the next poem "Earth's Answer," and who is the ill-tempered old man in the sky that results from our efforts to visualize a First Cause. Attempts to approach the Spirit directly produce the vague millennialism of the revolutionaries of Blake's time, where human nature as it exists is assumed to be perfectible at some time in the future. What Blake thinks of this he has expressed in the prose introduction to the third part of *Jerusalem*. For Blake there is no God but Jesus, who is also Man, and who exists neither in the past like the historical Jesus, nor in the future like the Jewish Messiah, but now in a real present, in which the real past and the real future are contained. The word "eternity" in Blake means the reality of the present moment, not the indefinite extension of the temporal sequence.

The modern poet or "Bard" thus finds himself in the tradition of the Hebrew prophets, who derive their inspiration from Christ as Word of God, and whose life is a listening for and speaking with that Word. In the Christian view, as recorded in *Paradise Lost*, it was not the Father but Jesus who created the unfallen world, placed man in Eden, and discovered man's fall while "walking in the garden in the cool of the day" (Gen. iii.8), the passage alluded to in the last line of the stanza.

> Calling the lapsed Soul,
> And weeping in the evening dew;
> That might controll
> The starry pole,
> And fallen, fallen light renew!

"Calling" refers primarily to Christ, the Holy Word calling Adam in the garden, and the "lapsed Soul" is presumably Adam, though the epithet seems curious, as Blake did not believe in a soul, but only in a spiritual body, as far as individual man is concerned. The word "weeping" also refers primarily to Christ. Neither in the Biblical story

nor in *Paradise Lost*, where we might expect it, do we get much sense of
Christ as deeply moved by man's fate, except in theory. Blake is making
a much more definite identification than Milton does of Adam's
"gracious judge, without revile" with the Jesus of the Gospels who wept
over the death of man as typified in Lazarus. Both the calling and the
weeping, of course, are repeated by the Bard; the denunciations of the
prophet and the elegiac vision of the poet of experience derive from
God's concern over fallen man.

In the last three lines the grammatical antecedent of "That" is
"Soul"; hence we seem to be told that man, if he had not fallen, would
have had the powers as well as the destiny of a god. He would not now
be subject to an involuntary subordination to a "nature" that alternately
freezes and roasts him. On a second look, however, we see that Blake is
not saying "might have controlled," but "might controll": the conquest
of nature is now within man's powers, and is a conquest to which the
poets and prophets are summoning him with the voice of the Word of
God. We are very close here to Blake's central doctrine of art, and the
reason for his insistence that "Jesus & his Apostles & Disciples were all
Artists."

The ordinary world that we see is a mindless chaos held together
by automatic order: an impressive ruin, but a "slumberous mass," and
not the world man wants to live in. What kind of world man wants to
live in is indicated by the kind of world he keeps trying to create: a city
and a garden. But his cities and gardens, unlike the New Jerusalem and
Eden of the Biblical revelation, are not eternal or infinite, nor are they
identical with the body of God. By "Artist" Blake means something
more like charitable man or man of visible love. He is the man who lives
now in the true world which is man's home, and tries to make that world
visible to others. "Let every Christian," urges Blake, "engage himself
openly & publicly before all the World in some Mental pursuit for the
Building up of Jerusalem."

The second stanza particularly illustrates the fact that what is true
of time must be equally true of space. Just as the real form of time is "A
vision of the Eternal Now," so the real form of space is "here." Again, in
ordinary experience of space, the center of space, which is "here," cannot
be located, except vaguely as within a certain area: all experienced space
is "there," which is why, when we invent such gods as Nobodaddy, we
place them "up there," in the sky and out of sight. But as "eternal" means

really present, so "infinite" means really here. Christ is a real presence in space as well as a real present in time, and the poet's imagination has the function of bringing into ordinary experience what is really here and now, the bodily presence of God. Just as there is no God except a God who is also Man, so there is no real man except Jesus, man who is also God. Thus the imagination of the poet, by making concrete and visible a hidden creative power, repeats the Incarnation.

If all times are now in the imagination, all spaces are here. Adam before his fall lived in a Paradisal garden, a garden which is to be one day restored to him, but which since his fall has existed, as Jesus taught, within us, no longer a place but a state of mind. Thus Blake begins *Milton* by speaking of his own brain as a part of the Garden of Eden, which his art attempts to realize in the world. In the Bible the Garden of Eden is the imaginative form of what existed in history as the tyrannies of Egypt and Babylon. Similarly the Promised Land, flowing with milk and honey, is the imaginative form of what existed historically as the theocracy of Israel. England, along with America, is also the historical form of what in the imagination is the kingdom of Atlantis, which included both, but now lies under the "Sea of Time and Space" flooding the fallen mind. We begin at this point to see the connection between our present poem and the famous lyric, written much later as a preface to *Milton*, "And did those feet in ancient time." As all imaginative places are the same place, Atlantis, Eden, and the Promised Land are the same place; hence when Christ walked in the Garden of Eden in the cool of the day he was also walking on the spiritual form of England's mountains green, among the "Druid" oaks. We note that Blake speaks in the first line of his poem not of a poet or a prophet but of a "Bard," in his day an almost technical term for a tradition of *British* poets going back to the dawn of history. "All had originally one · language, and one religion: this was the religion of Jesus, the Everlasting Gospel."

> O Earth, O Earth, return!
> Arise from out the dewy grass;
> Night is worn,
> And the morn
> Rises from the slumberous mass.

The first words spoken by Jesus through the mouth of his "Bard" are, appropriately enough, quoted from the Hebrew prophets. The first line refers partly to the desperate cry of Jeremiah faced with the invincible stupidity of his king: "O earth, earth, earth, hear the word of the Lord!" (Jer. xxii.29). A century earlier Milton, after twenty years spent in defending the liberty of the English people, helplessly watching them choose "a Captain back for Egypt," could express himself only in the same terms, in a passage at the end of *The Ready and Easy Way* that may have focused Blake's attention on his source:

> Thus much I should perhaps have said, though I were sure I should have spoken only to Trees and Stones; and had none to cry to, but with the Prophet, *O Earth, Earth, Earth!* to tell the very Soil itself, what her perverse inhabitants are deaf to.

There is also an echo in the same line from Isaiah (xxi.11–12):

> He calleth to me out of Seir, Watchman, what of the night? Watchman, what of the night? The watchman said, The morning cometh, and also the night: if ye will inquire, inquire ye: return, come.

Both in the Hebrew language and in Blake's, "cometh" could also be rendered by "has come": the light and the darkness are simultaneously with us, one being "here" and the other "there," one trying to shine from within, the other surrounding us. Hence a third Biblical allusion appears dimly but firmly attached to the other two (John i.5): "And the light shineth in darkness; and the darkness comprehended it not." The "fallen light," therefore, is the alternating light and darkness of the world we know; the unfallen light would be the eternal light of the City of God, where there is no longer need for sun or moon, and where we can finally see, as Blake explains in the prophecies, that no creative act of man has, in fact, really disappeared in time.

We notice in this stanza that the "Soul" is now identified, not as Adam, but as "Earth," a being who, as we can see by a glance at the next poem, is female. Thus the "Soul" is a kind of *anima mundi*; she includes not only the individual man and the "Church" but the totality of life, the whole creation that, as Paul says, groaneth and travaileth in pain together until now. She is also Nature red in tooth and claw, the struggle for existence in the animal world, of which man, in his fallen aspect, forms part. The prophet sees in every dawn the image of a resurrection that will lift the world into another state of being altogether. He is always prepared to say "the time is at hand." But every dawn in the world "out there" declines into sunset, as the spinning earth turns away into darkness.

> Turn away no more;
> Why wilt thou turn away?
> The starry floor,
> The wat'ry shore,
> Is giv'n thee till the break of day.

There are two ways of looking at the "fallen" world: as fallen, and as a protection against worse things. Man might conceivably have fallen into total chaos, or nonexistence, or, like Tithonus or Swift's Struldbrugs, he might have been forced to live without the hope of death. This world is pervaded by a force that we call natural law, and natural law, however mindless and automatic, at any rate affords a solid bottom to life: it provides a sense of the predictable and trustworthy on which the imagination may build. The role of natural law (called Bowlahoola in the prophecies) as the basis of imaginative effort is what Blake has in mind when he calls creation "an act of Mercy"; the providential aspect of time, in sweeping everything away into an apparent nonexistence, is brought out in his observation that "Time is the Mercy of Eternity." In the Bible a similar sense of the created world as a protection against chaos, usually symbolized in the Bible by the sea, as a firmament in the midst of the waters, comes out in the verse in Job (xxxviii.11): "Hitherto shalt thou come but no further, and here shall thy proud waves be stayed." It is this verse that Blake has in mind when he speaks of the "wat'ry shore" as given to Earth until the Last Judgment; it is the same guarantee that God gave to Noah in the figure of the rainbow. Similarly the automatic accuracy of the heavenly bodies, of which Earth of course is one, affords a minimum basis for imaginative effort. Newtonian science is quite acceptable to Blake as long as it deals with the automatism of nature as the "floor" and not the ceiling of experience.

In Blake's prophecies there are two perspectives, so to speak, on human life. One is a tragic and ironic vision; the other sees life as part of a redemptive divine comedy. The usual form taken by the tragic vision is that of a cyclical narrative, seen at its fullest and clearest in *The Mental Traveller* and *The Gates of Paradise*. Here there are two main characters, a male figure, the narrator in *The Gates of Paradise* and the "Boy" of *The Mental Traveller*, and a female figure who, in the latter poem, grows younger as the male grows older and vice versa, and who in *The Gates of Paradise* is described as "Wife, Sister, Daughter, to the Tomb."

The "Boy" of *The Mental Traveller* is struggling humanity, called Orc in the prophecies. The female figure is nature, which human culture partially but never completely subdues in a series of historical cycles. The relations between them are roughly those of mother and son, wife and husband, daughter and father. Very roughly, for none of these relations is quite accurate: the mother is an old nurse, the wife merely a temporary possession, and the daughter a changeling. The "Female will," as Blake calls it, has no necessary connection with human women, who are part of humanity, except when a woman wants to make a career of being a "harlot coy," or acting as nature does. The female will is rather the elusive, retreating, mysterious remoteness of the external world.

The "Introduction" to the *Songs of Experience*, despite its deeply serious tone, takes on the whole the redemptive or providential view. Hence the relation of the two figures is reversed, or rather, as they are not the same figures, the relation of a male and a female figure is used to symbolize the redemption of man instead of his bondage. The two characters correspond to the Bridegroom and Bride of Biblical symbolism. The male character is primarily Christ or the Word of God, which extends to take in the prophets and poets, and is ultimately Christ as the creative power in the whole of humanity. The "Bard" is called Los in the prophecies, the Holy Spirit who proceeds from the Son. The female character Earth embraces everything that Christ is trying to redeem, the forgiven harlot of the Old Testament prophets who keeps turning away from forgiveness. She has no name, as such, in the prophecies, though her different aspects have different names, the most important being Ahania and Enion. She is in general what Blake calls the "emanation," the total form of what man, or rather God in man, is trying to create. This total form, a city, a garden, a home, and a bed of love, or as Blake says "a City, yet a Woman," is Jerusalem. But just as the female will is. not necessarily human women, so Earth, the Bride of Christ, includes. men, as in the more conventional symbol of the Church.

In her "Answer" Earth rejects with bitterness and some contempt the optimistic tone of the Bard's final words. She does not feel protected; she feels imprisoned, in the situation dramatized in Blake's poem *Visions of the Daughters of Albion*. She recalls Io, guarded by the myriad-eyed Argus, or Andromeda, chained on the seashore and constantly devoured by a possessive jealousy. Earth is not saying, as some critics accuse her of saying, that all would be well if lovers would only learn to copulate in the daytime. She is saying that nearly all of man's creative life remains embryonic, shrouded in darkness, on the level of wish, hope, dream, and private fantasy. Man is summoned by the Bard to love the world and let his love shine before men, but his natural tendency, as a child of fallen nature, is the miser's tendency to associate love with some private and secret possession of his own. This "dark secret love," or rather perversion of love, is what Blake means by jealousy.

The "Selfish father of men" who keeps Earth imprisoned is not God the Father, of course, but the false father that man visualizes as soon as he takes his mind off the Incarnation. To make God a Father is to make ourselves children: if we do this in the light of the Gospels, we see the world in the light of the state of innocence. But if we take the point of view of the child of ordinary experience, our God becomes a protection of ordinary childishness, a vision of undeveloped humanity. If we think of God as sulky, capricious, irritable, and mindlessly cruel, like Dante's primal love who made hell, or tied in knots of legal quibbles, like Milton's father-god, we may have a very awful divinity, but we have not got a very presentable human being. There is no excuse for keeping such a creature around when we have a clear revelation of God's human; nature in the Gospels.

The source of this scarecrow is fallen nature: man makes a gigantic idol out of the dark world, and is so impressed by its stupidity, cruelty, empty spaces, and automatism that he tries to live in accordance with the dreary ideals it suggests. He naturally assumes that his god is jealous of everything he clings to with secret longing and wants it surrendered to, him; hence he develops a religion of sacrifice. There are two other reasons for Earth's calling her tormentor the "father of the ancient men." In the first place, he is the ghost of what in the New Testament would be called the first Adam. In the second place, he is the god to whom the "Druids" sacrificed human beings in droves, as an eloquent symbol of their belief, quite true in itself, that their god hated human life. This false father still exists as the shadow thrown by Newtonian science into the stars, or what Blake calls the "Spectre." He is the genius of discouragement, trying to impress us with the reality of the world of experience and the utter unreality of anything better. His chief weapons are moral conformity, sexual shame, and the kind of rationality that always turns out to be anti-intellectual. If we could only get rid of him, "every thing would appear to man as it is, infinite."

In the three characters of these two poems we have the three generating forces, so to speak, of all Blake's symbolism. First is the Bard, representative of the whole class that Blake in *Milton* calls "Reprobate," personified by Los, and including all genuine prophets and artists. They are given this name because their normal social role is that of a persecuted and ridiculed minority. Earth includes the total class of the "Redeemed," or those capable of responding to the Reprobate. In the later prophecies Blake tends to use the masculine and purely human symbol of "Albion" as representing what the prophet tries to redeem. We can see part of the reason for this change in the poems we are studying: the Bard appeals to Earth, but Earth reminds him that man is responsible for his own evils, and that he should talk only to man if he is to do anything to help her.

The father of the ancient men is what in *Milton* is called the "Elect," because the idolatry of fallen nature incarnates itself in all natural societies; that is, the tyrannies of warriors and priests. In *Milton* too the Reprobate and Redeemed are called "Contraries," because the conflict between them is the "Mental fight" in which every man is obligated to engage. The Elect constitutes a "Negation": he is the aspect of the law that the Gospel annihilates, as distinct from the "starry floor," or basis of imaginative order which it fulfills.

NOTES

1. William Blake: A Critical Essay (London, 1906), p. 140.

2. Letter to Trusler in Geoffrey Keynes, *The Complete Writings of William Blake* (London, 1957), p. 794. All subsequent page references in the text to Blake's works will be to this edition, though for the major works under discussion I shall retain consistently Blake's punctuation rather than Keynes's.

3. *William Blake: A Critical Study*, p. 140.

4. *Ibid.*, p. 161.

5. There has been considerable discussion about how much of his system Blake derived from others, particularly Boehme, Swedenborg, and various neo-Platonists. The ideas of a primal unity, a fall into division, and a return to unity are of course not new, and no one can deny that there are many isolated instances of congeniality between Blake and various philosophers, theologians, pseudo-scientists, Gnostics, Cabbalists, and so forth. In none of them, however, is there an adumbration of Blake's system as I shall define it, except insofar as many of their symbols turn up in Blake's poetry. Even here Blake's mind did with them what it would, and my occasional references to a "source" are more as an aid to clarification than a suggestion of indebtedness. That Blake's system only gradually developed, with many fits and starts, is adequate proof of its essential originality. For the controversy over the influence of other writers see especially Mark Schorer, *William Blake: The Politics of Vision* (New York, 1946), pp. 104–148; J.G. Davies, *The Theology of William Blake* (Oxford, 1948), pp. 35–49; Paul Berger, *William Blake: Poet and Mystic*, trans. Danid H. Connor (New York, 1915), pp. 13, 55, 57, 198–208, 211–220; Helen C. White, *The Mysticism of William Blake* (Madison, 1927), pp. 128–164; David V. Erdman, *William Blake: Prophet against Empire* (Princeton, 1956), *passim*; and a group of scattered articles and essays by George Mills Harper and Kathleen Raine.

6. Blake never uses the former term in this sense, but for his use of the latter see *The First Book of Urizen*, 227 (hereafter referred to as *Urizen*).

7. *The Four Zoas*, 277, hereafter referred to as *Zoas*.

8. "To the Jews," *Jerusalem*, 649.

9. *Milton*, 483. Cf. *Zoas*, 264:
Four Mighty Ones are in every Man; a Perfect Unity
Cannot Exist but from the Universal Brotherhood of Eden,
The Universal Man....

10. Letter to Butts, 805. Cf. *A Vision of the Last Judgment*, 605-606, and especially the Annotations to Lavater's *Aphorisms*, 87.

11. See, e.g., *Zoas*, 374; *Jerusalem*, 664–665.

12. Annotations to Swedenborg, 89.

13. *Literature and the Occult Tradition*, trans. Dorothy Bolton (London, 1930), pp. 17–18.

14. Annotations to Lavater, 83; Annotations to Swedenborg, 90.

15. *The Marriage of Heaven and Hell*, 151, hereafter cited as *Marriage*.

16. See Blake's Annotations to Lavater, 77 (no. 409) and 88 (no. 640). See also *Last Judgment*, 615, par. 2.

17. Annotations to Reynolds, 471; Letter to Trusler, 794; Annotations to Reynolds, 473.

18. *Last Judgment*, 604. In this work is a good example of what Blake probably meant by "spiritual sensation." Speaking of his painting of the Last Judgment he says: "If the Spectator could Enter into these Images in his Imagination, approaching them on the Fiery Chariot of his Contemplative Thought, if he could Enter into Noah's Rainbow or into his bosom, or could make a Friend & Companion of one of these Images of wonder, which always intreats him to leave mortal things (as he must know), then would he arise from his Grave [i.e., this world], then would he meet the Lord in the Air & then he would be happy" (611). See also Chapter III of this study for an examination of Blake's technique as an application of his theory of the symbolic imagination.

19. Annotations to Wordsworths' *Poems*, 783; Annotations to Berkeley's *Siris*, 775; *Last Judgment*, 617.

20. This is what Blake scrupulously avoided in all of his work. In one place he wrote: "'What,' it will be Question'd, 'When the Sun rises, do you not see a round disk of fire somewhat like a Guinea?' 0 no, no, I see an Innumerable company of the Heavenly host crying, 'Holy, Holy, Holy is the Lord God Almighty.' I question not my Corporeal or Vegetative Eye any more than I would Question a Window concerning a Sight. I look thro' it & not with it" (*Last Judgment*, 617). Cf. *Auguries of Innocence*, 433–434, lines 125–128.

21. *The Delights of Wisdom Pertaining to Conjugial Love after which Follow The Pleasures of Insanity Pertaining to Scortatory Love* (New York, 1910), p. 157, par. 143.

22. *The Everlasting Gospel*, 748–759. See also *Marriage*, 158.

23. I use the word "reorganize" here advisedly since Blake insisted, "unorganiz'd Innocence: An Impossibility. Innocence dwells with Wisdom, but never with Ignorance" (Notes written on a page of *Zoas*, 380). Cf. *Zoas*, 366, lines 363–374.

24. *William Blake's Circle of Destiny* (New York, 1938), pp. 123–124. See Blake's *Everlasting Gospel*, 753–757.

25. *William Blake: The Politics of Vision*, p. 268.

26. *A Man without a Mask* (London, 1947), p. 135.

27. *William Blake's Circle of Destiny*, pp. 11–12.

28. *Heaven and Its Wonders, the World of Spirits, and Hell: From Things Heard and Seen*, trans. Rev. Samuel Noble (New York 1864), p. 134, par. 278.

29. *Poetry and Myth* (New York, 1927), p. 173.

30. Ellis and Yeats define this idea with admirable precision: Urizen falls "into chaos, which is memory, because memory is the record of the merely egoistic experience, thus differing from inspiration, which is direct experience."—*The Works of William Blake* (3 vols., London, 1893), I, 252.

31. *The Everlasting Gospel*, 750; statement by Lavater, underlined by Blake and called "ture worship" (82).

32. *An Introduction to the Study of Blake* (London, 1927), p. 133.

33. *Heaven and Its Wonders ... and Hell*, p. 9, par. 15; p. 13, par. 23; *Concerning the Earths in Our Solar System which Are Called Planets*, trans. anon. (London, 1787), pp. 116–117.

34. *Marriage*, 158. Swedenborg could never hold such a view as this, since he never identified the evil man with the all-good God. Indeed he probably would have reacted to this statement in the *Marriage* much as the angel did when he heard Blake's devil speak the words: "The Angel hearing this became almost blue but mastering himself he grew yellow, & at last white pink & smiling. and then replied, Thou Idolater, is not God One? & is not he visible in Jesus Christ? and has not Jesus Christ given his sanction to the law of ten commandments and are not all other men fools. sinners & nothings."

35. See, e.g., *Urizen*, 235–236; *The Book of Ahania*, 255; *Zoas*, 374; *Milton*, 517–518; *Jerusalem*, 679–680, 724–725.

W.J.T. MITCHELL

Blake's Composite Art

The illuminated poetry of William Blake presents a unique problem in the interpretation of the arts, for although there have been many artists who have worked in several different media, rarely do we find one equally renowned in more than one field, and even more rarely do we encounter an artist who can successfully combine several art forms. Michelangelo's sonnets would not be read if he had not carved in marble, and Wagner's libretti survive, not for their inherent value, but because of their musical settings. Blake's "sister arts" of poetry and painting, on the other hand, have survived at least a century of misunderstanding without the mutual support of one another. In the twentieth century his paintings and etchings have risen in market value to equal and surpass those of his formerly better known contemporaries, and the bare words of his poetry have appeared in edition after edition. Until recently, Blake's two arts have gone their separate ways in criticism as well, with only occasional bursts of cross fire between the art historians and the literary critics. Today, however, the question is no longer *whether* Blake's poetry and painting have anything to do with one another, but *how* their relationship may best be understood.

Since the two sides of Blake's genius have made their ways in the world without the help of one another, it is proper to ask what is gained by yoking them together. Suzanne Langer's observation that there are no marriages of the arts, only successful rapes, must serve as a warning to

From *Blake's Visionary Forms Dramatic*, pp. 57–81. David V. Erdman and John E. Grant, ed. © 1970 by Princeton University Press.

anyone who would deflower either of Blake's arts for the sake of elucidating the other. It is one thing to say that one form helps to explain or amplify the other; quite another to claim (as this essay does) that the illuminated poems constitute a composite art, a single, unified aesthetic phenomenon in which neither form dominates the other and yet in which each is incomplete without the other.

There may be a kind of ironic virtue, then, in the long period of division that Blake's composite art has undergone. If, as seems apparent from the tendencies of the present volume,[1] the next major step in Blake studies is to be a critical reunification of text and design, it will be important to remind ourselves of how well the two art forms have done on their own, and to account for this fact even as we bring them together. The word "illustration," for instance, will have to be redefined when applied to Blake. It will simply not do to say that his designs illustrate the text if we mean only that they throw light upon, explicate, or provide a visual rendition of matters which have been sufficiently expounded in the text. If this were an adequate definition, it would be very difficult to explain the fact that Anthony Blunt has been able to write a very fine study of the paintings on the assumption that they are completely superior to the poems (especially the later prophecies), and that the text is in reality only a kind of pretext for the real art in the designs.[2] The poetry, thanks to the endless vocabularies of literary critics, will take care of itself; but the art is in danger of being infected by the concept of illustration. As a kind of verbal prophylactic, therefore, it might be appropriate at the outset to remind ourselves that when Blake "illustrates" a text, he expands and transforms it, and often provides a vision which can operate in complete separation from it.

Blake's reluctance to permit this separation has often been remarked. In referring to a friend's request for separate plates from *The Marriage of Heaven and Hell, The Book of Urizen*, and several other minor prophecies, he objected strongly: "Those I Printed ... are a selection from the different Books of such as could be Printed without the Writing, tho' to the Loss of some of the best things. For they, when Printed perfect, accompany Poetical Personifications & Acts, without which Poems they never could have been Executed."[3] It is interesting to note, however, that a substantial number of the designs he sent to his friend do *not* illustrate specifically any of the "Poetical Personifications & Acts" in the poems to which they were attached.[4] It is no accident that amid all the meticulous Blake scholarship that has appeared in recent years, there is still no authoritative index or commentary identifying the subjects of his illustrations.[5] In *The Songs of Innocence and of Experience*, of course, the problem of specification of content is greatly simplified by the direct juxtaposition of the design with a limited text, but even in the case of these poems (especially *Experience*) there are problems. In the longer prophetic works, however, the relationship becomes very attenuated: illustrations often seem purposely placed as far as possible from their textual reference—when there is a reference to be found at all. As Blake increased his mastery of both poetic and pictorial techniques, it seems that he tended to minimize the literal, denotative correspondences between the two forms.

There is no difficulty in locating a context for composite art forms in Blake's intellectual milieu. The eighteenth century was, after all, the age which discovered that art could be spelled with a capital A, and Abbé Batteaux could title his 1746 treatise *Les Beaux Arts reduits à un même principe*.[6] Book illustration was expanding into a minor industry, and individual poems such as Thomson's *Seasons* were illustrated so often that it has been possible for one modern critic to construct a history of late-eighteenth-century criticism largely on the basis of the illustrations of this one poem.[7] Since the Renaissance an elaborate apologetics had developed around the illustrated book, especially the emblem book, taking the Horatian maxim *ut pictura poesis* for its central principle.[8] The critical dogmas which calcified around Horace's innocent phrase had already provoked an adverse reaction from Lessing,[9] however, and we should be surprised to find an independent mind like Blake's receiving them passively.

The two basic premises of the doctrine of *ut pictura poesis* were, first, that all art is to be understood as a species of imitation, and second, that the reality which is to be imitated is essentially dualistic. The personification of poetry and painting as the "sister arts" was no accident; it expressed concisely the eighteenth century's conviction that the two arts were daughters of the Nature which they imitated, and that they provided complementary representations of a dualistic world of space and time,[10] body and *soul, dulce et utile*,[11] sense and intellect.[12] The emblem book enjoyed a particularly privileged position because it not only fulfilled the classical ideal of uniting the arts, but also could be seen as a means of providing the most comprehensive possible imitation of a bifurcated reality. "The emblem," as Jean Hagstrum points out, "seemed to be the completest and most satisfying form of expression imaginable, since body (the picture) and soul (the verse) were vitally connected."[13] Painting was supposed to appeal to the senses, poetry to the intellect, and the union of the two arts, it was presumed, would counteract that "dissociated sensibility" which T.S. Eliot had not yet invented. Cesare Ripa, perhaps the most important of the emblematists, plagiarized Marino to affirm that the union of the arts "causes us almost to understand with the senses, ... to feel with the intellect."[14] An even more extravagant claim was made by the anonymous essayist of *The Plain Dealer* in 1724: "*Two Sister Arts*, uniting their different Powers, the one transmitting *Souls*, the other *Bodies* (or the outward Form of Bodies) their combining Influence would be of Force to frustrate *Death itself*: And all the ages of the World would seem to be Contemporaries."[15]

Blake's critique of the implications of *ut pictura poesis* can be understood most clearly in terms of his reception of the idea of Nature assumed by this doctrine. For Blake, the dualistic world of mind and body, time and space, is an illusion which must not be imitated, but which must be dispelled by the processes of his art: "But first the notion that a man has a body distinct from his soul, is to be expunged; this I shall do by printing in the infernal method, by corrosives, melting apparent surfaces away, and displaying the infinite which was hid" (*MHH* 14). The methods of relief etching here become a metaphor for the destruction of the appearance of dualism. Blake would agree with the attempt of the emblematists to unite the two arts, not, however, as a means of representing the full range of reality, but as a means of exposing as a fiction the bifurcated organization of that reality. The separation of body and soul, space and time, Blake sees as various manifestations of the fall of man, "His fall into Division" (*FZ* I 4:4). The function of his composite art is therefore twofold: it must "melt apparent surfaces away" by exposing the errors and contradictions of dualism; and it must display "the infinite which was hid," and overcome the "fall into division" with a "Resurrection to Unity" (*FZ* I 4:4).

Blake never refers to his painting and poetry as "the sister arts," a curious omission for a man who lived at the end of the age which had systematized this relationship so carefully. The reason lies in his conception of the nature of the dualities that his art was designed to overcome. Blake's most pervasive metaphor for the "fall into Division" is the separation of the sexes. In particular, the apparent division of the world into space and time is described as a sexual antinomy: "Time & Space are Real Beings, a Male & a Female. Time is a Man, Space is a Woman" (*VLJ* E553/K614). In Blake's myth, the sexes do not exist as part of the ultimate reality, but are the product of pride and egotism: "When the Individual appropriates Universality / He divides into Male & Female" (*J* 90:51–52). The danger is, according to Blake, that this sexual polarity will be mistaken for the final nature of things: "when the Male & Female / Appropriate Individuality, they become an Eternal Death" (*J* 90:52–53). That is, in terms of space and time, when space becomes an individual, an end in itself, it becomes a prison-house, the "Mundane Shell" of matter which is mistakenly supposed to be independent of consciousness. In like manner, time becomes a nonhuman phenomenon, an endless Heraclitean flux or the "dull round" of a fatal, mechanistic determinism. Blake's poetry and painting must begin by invalidating these incontingent views of time and space, and end by replacing them with visions of eternity and infinity. His primary disagreement with eighteenth-century conceptions of composite art, then, is that they presuppose an incontingent Nature which is to be copied and represented in a complementary, additive manner. For Blake, the coupling of poetry and painting is desirable not because it will produce a fuller range of imitation, but because it can dramatize the interaction of the apparent dualities in experience, and because it can embody the strivings of those dualities for unification.

If we conceive of text and design as Blake did, as organized expressions of the polarized phenomena of space and time, their relationship becomes intelligible in terms of his theory of contrariety. If a purpose of his art is to dramatize the struggle of the antinomies of our experience into a unified vision, the vehicles of spatial and temporal form must embody this dialectic as well. Regarded in this way, the separation of text and design can be seen as having two functions. First, it has a hermeneutic function, in that the disparity between poem and illustration entices the mind of the reader to supply the missing connections. In this light, the illuminated book serves as an "Allegory address'd to the Intellectual Powers" which is "fittest for Instruction because it rouzes the faculties to act."[16] Second, the separation has a mimetic function, in that the contrariety of poem and picture reflects the world of the reader as a place of apparent separation of temporal and spatial, mental and physical phenomena.

It is important to remember the adjective "apparent" when talking about the discrepancies between Blake's designs and text, however, for if we are correct, the most disparate pictorial and verbal structures must conceal a subtle identity of significance. The title page of *The Marriage of Heaven and Hell* {3} exemplifies the way in which the apparent unrelatedness of content in design and text belies the close affinities of formal arrangement. A pair of nudes embrace in a subterranean scene at the bottom of the page, the one on the left emerging from flames, the one on the right from clouds. The top of the page is framed by a pair of trees, between which are two sets of human figures. No scene in the poem corresponds to this picture,[17] and yet it is a perfect representation of the poem's theme, the marriage of contraries:

> Without Contraries is no progression. Attraction and Re-
> pulsion, Reason and Energy, Love and Hate, are necessary to
> Human Existence.
> From these contraries spring what the religious call Good
> & Evil. Good is the passive that obeys Reason. Evil is the
> active springing from Energy.
> Good is Heaven. Evil is Hell.
>
> (*MHH* 3)

Every aspect of the composition is deployed to present this vision of contraries: flames versus clouds, red versus blue, the aggressive inward thrust of the female flying up from the left versus the receptive outward pose of the figure on the right. At the top, the trees on the left reach their branches across to the right, while the trees on the right recoil into themselves. The couple beneath the trees on the left walk hand in hand toward the right. The couple on the right face away, and are separated, one kneeling, the other lying on the ground. This last detail suggests that the composition is not simply a visual blending of contraries, but also a statement about their relative value. The active side presents a harmonious vision of the sexes; the passive, an inharmonious division, in which the male seems to be trying to woo the female from her indifference by playing on a musical instrument.[18] This tipping of the balance in favor of the "Devil's Party" is accentuated by the direction of movement that pervades the whole design. If we were simply to have a balanced presentation of contraries such as the text suggests, we would expect a simple symmetrical arrangement, with a vertical axis down the center (see fig. 2a). But, in fact, the whole kinesis of the composition, accentuated by the flying nudes in the center, produces an axis which goes from the lower left corner to the upper right. If one were to draw vectors indicating the probable course of the figures in the center of the design, the result would be the diagonal axis of figure 2b.

This tilting of the symmetry of the contraries, is, of course, exactly what happens to the theme of the *Marriage* as Blake treats it. Although the contraries are theoretically equal, Blake has all his fun by identifying himself with the side of the devils. The poem is not simply a self-contained dialectic; it is a dialogue with Blake's own time, and he felt that the "Angels" already had plenty of spokesmen, such as Swedenborg and the apologists for traditional religion and morality. At his particular historical moment, Blake felt that the axis needed to be tilted in favor of energy. Hence, all the good lines in the work and the advantageous pictorial treatments are reserved for the representatives of Hell. But the style of lettering in the title page returns us to the theoretical equality which Blake sees between the contraries. Both "Heaven" and "Hell" are printed in rather stark block letters; the flamboyant, energetic style of free-flowing lines and swirls is reserved for the key term in the poem, "Marriage."

Blake's departure from the literalist implications of *ut pictura poesis* was not, however, simply confined to the avoidance, in his own work, of mere illustration. The doctrine also had implications for the nature of poetry and painting in general, apart from their employment in a composite form like the illustrated book. The concept of the ideal unity of the arts was used to encourage, on the one hand, "painterly," descriptive poetry like Thomson's, and on the other, "poetical," literary painting like Hogarth's. Poetry was to become pictorial by evoking a flood of images which could be reconstituted in the reader's mind into a detailed scene. Painting was to become poetical by imitating a significant action, with beginning, middle, and end,[19] not just a fleeting moment, and by representing not only the surfaces of things but also the interior passions and characters of men. Each art was expected to transcend its temporal or spatial limitation by moving toward the condition of its sister.

This conception of the unification of the arts can only be applied very meagerly to Blake's practice. His poetry, like Milton's, avoids "painterly" descriptions in favor of visual paradoxes like "darkness visible" and "the hapless Soldiers sigh" which "Runs in blood down Palace walls." When he does have an opportunity for "iconic" passages describing a fixed object, such as the building of the art-city of Golgonooza in *Jerusalem*, the result is anything but a set of visualizable images:

> The great City of Golgonooza: fourfold toward the north
> And toward the south fourfold & fourfold toward the east
>   & west
> Each within other toward the four points: that toward
> Eden, and that toward the World of Generation,
> And that toward Beulah, and that toward Ulro:
> Ulro is the space of the terrible starry wheels of Albions sons:
> But that toward Eden is walled up, till time of renovation:
> Yet it is perfect in its building, ornaments & perfection.
>   (*J* 12:46–53)

It is no accident that Blake, for all his ability to visualize the unseen, never illustrated this passage. In fact his prophetic illustrations generally do not provide visual equivalents for specific passages, but often expand upon some point of only minor importance in the text, or even convey an opposed or ironic vision.

Blake's refusal to illustrate an "iconic" passage such as the description of Golgonooza is a clue, moreover, to the extent of his departure from the tradition of "literary" painting. Architectural backgrounds, the standard setting of the history painting, naturally generated a more or less "objective" and mathematically constructed spatial container for the human form. But Blake, who considered himself a history painter (see the subtitle of his *Descriptive Catalogue*) could hardly be more perfunctory in his treatment of this kind of subject matter. He is interested not in the mechanically determined form of the material city but in its spiritual (i.e., human) form, as in *Jerusalem* 57, where he specifies the cities of York, London, and Jerusalem with tiny geographical emblems (fig. 18), but defines them pictorially as gigantic women. Jerusalem, particularly, while both a city and a woman in the text, is primarily a woman in the illustrations.

Blake's rejection of the architectural background is only one symptom of his general refusal to employ very extensively the techniques of three-dimensional illusionism which had been increasingly perfected since the Renaissance.[20] This kind of illusionism was particularly popular with "literary" painters, since it provided an easy metaphor for the temporal structure of the scene being depicted. The earliest event in the narrative could be placed in the foreground, and the later events could be placed in increasingly distant perspective planes.[21] Blake avoids this kind of illusionism in his designs for his own works. As a rule, he concentrates on a few foreground images, often arranged symmetrically, to encourage an instantaneous grasp of the whole design rather than an impression of dramatic sequence. Sometimes, to be sure, he does present metamorphic sequences across the foreground plane, usually in his marginal designs, where (for obvious reasons) radial and bilateral symmetry must give way to some kind of linear presentation. These mural-like tableaux, however, embody the passage of time not as a progression from the near to the distant, or the clear to the obscure, but as a movement from the near to the near. All moments in the sequence are immediate and "immanent"; just as in the poetry, the prophet-narrator "present, past, & future *sees*" as an eternal *now*.

The other desideratum of "poetical" painting, the representation of the interior life of its human subjects, not just their outward features, likewise seems inapplicable to Blake's practice. His human figures have a kind of allegorical anonymity, and are clearly designed as types, not as subtly differentiated portraits. We see very little subjectivity in the faces of Blake's figures for the same reason we do not find "motivation" or novelistic personalities in his poetical personifications. Urizen cannot have his own interior life like the character of a novel; he is only an aspect of the interior life of the single human mind which constitutes the world of his poem. Blake certainly expresses the passions in his painting: but he does not present them as residing *within* particular human figures; he presents them as human figures. His portraits are not of men with minds, but of the mind itself.

The methods of pictorialist poetry and literary painting, then, shed only a negative light on the specific manner in which Blake approaches the problem of unifying the arts. He rejects the practice of mutual transference of techniques in favor of a methodology which seems rather to emphasize the peculiar strengths and limitations of each medium: the shadowy, allusive metamorphoses of language, and the glowing fixity of almost abstract pictorial forms.

In Blake's view, the attempt to make poetry visual and to make pictures "speak" and tell a story was bound to fail because it presumed the independent reality of space and time and treated them as the irreducible foundations of existence. As we have seen, Blake considers space and time, like the sexes, to be contraries whose reconciliation occurs not when one becomes like the other, but when they approach a condition in which these categories cease to function. In the simplest possible terms, his poetry exists to invalidate the idea of objective time, his painting to invalidate the idea of objective space. To state this positively, his poetry affirms the power of the human imagination to create and organize time in its own image, and his painting affirms the centrality of the human body as the structural principle of space. The essential unity of his arts, then, is to be seen in the parallel engagements of imagination and body with their respective media, and in their convergence in the more comprehensive idea of the "Human Form Divine." For Blake, in the final analysis the body and the imagination are separable principles only in a fallen world of limited perception; the business of art is to dramatize their unification: "The Eternal Body of Man is The Imagination.... It manifests itself in his Works of Art" (*Laocoön*: E271).

Blake's specific techniques for constructing his art forms as critiques of their own media are quite clear. In the poetry he creates a world of process and metamorphosis in which the only stable, fixed term is the imagining and perceiving mind. Cause and effect, linear temporality, and other "objective" temporal structures for narrative are replaced by an imaginative conflation of all time in the pregnant moment. The prophetic narrator-actor perceives "Present, Past & Future" simultaneously, and is able to see in any given moment the structure of all history: "Every Time less than a pulsation of the artery / Is equal in its period & value to Six Thousand Years" (*M* 28:62–63). Consequently, the narrative order of the poem need not refer to any incontingent, nonhuman temporal continuum. Most narrative structures employ what Blake would call "twofold vision": that is, the imaginative arrangement of episodes is always done with reference to an "objective" time scheme. The narrative selects its moments and their order in terms of some imaginative order: *in medias res, ab ovum,* or *recherche du temps perdu.* All of these selective principles assume, however, that there is an order of nonhuman, "objective," or "real" time which flows onward independent of any human, "subjective," or "imaginary" reorganization of its sequence. For Blake, this objective temporal understructure is an illusion which is to be dispelled by the form of his poetry. The beginning, middle, and end of any action are all contained in the present; so the order of presentation is completely subject to the imagination of the narrator. Hostile critics have always recognized this quality in Blake's major prophecies when they indicted them for being "impossible to follow." That is precisely the point. Blake's prophecies go nowhere in time because time, as a linear, homogeneous phenomenon, has no place in their structure. *Jerusalem* is essentially a nonconsecutive series of poetic "happenings," not a linear ordering of events. The one continuous and stable element in the course of the narrative is the idea of consciousness as a transformer of itself and its world. That is why Los, the vehicle of the imagination, is also cast as the personification of time. In this way, Blake could depict the poet's management of time and the prophet's quarrel with history as the struggle of the individual with himself.

An analogous technique can be observed in the whole range of Blake's paintings. Historical parallels have tended to confuse attempts at defining Blake's style because the historical concept always carries with it a freight of alien associations which have no relevance to the work at hand. His art has recognizable affinities with Michelangelo, Raphael, and the Mannerists in his treatment of the human figure, with Gothic painting in his primitivism and anti-illusionism, and with contemporaries such as Flaxman in his stress on outline, Fuseli in his use of the terrific and exotic. It is also clear, however, that these elements are transmuted into something unified and unique in Blake's hands. His art is a curious compound of the representational and the abstract, the picture that imitates natural forms and the design that delights in form for its own sake. The "flame-flowers" which are so ubiquitous in his margins, and which later provided inspiration for art nouveau, serve as a prime example of the interplay between representation and abstraction that informs all his work. The abstract vorticular composition may assume specific representational form as a whirlpool, a dance of lovers, or a spiral ascent to the heavens. The circle may serve as the structural skeleton of the mathematical enclosures of Urizen, or of the glowing sun created by the hammer of Los. Plate 39 [44] of *Jerusalem* makes this technique explicit by showing a serpent metamorphosing into a flame, then a leaf, and finally the tendrils of a vine. The effect of this pictorial strategy is to undercut the representational appearance of particular forms and to endow them with an abstract, stylized existence independent of the natural images that they evoke. Pictorial form is freed from the labor of accurately representing any idea of nature, and instead serves to show that the appearances of natural objects are arbitrary and subject to transformation by the imagination. All art, of course, even that which claims only to provide a mirror image of external reality, transforms its subject matter in some way. But the subject of Blake's art is precisely this power to transform, this ability of the artist to reshape and control his visual images, and, by implication, the ability of man to create his vision in general. That is why at the center of Blake's visual world of process and metamorphosis the form of the human body tends to retain its uniqueness and stability. The backgrounds of Blake's designs, his landscapes and prospects, all serve as a kind of evanescent setting for the human form. There are no mathematically determined perspectives, and very few landscapes which would make any sense without the human figures they contain. Pictorial space does not exist independently as a uniform, objective container of forms; it exists to provide contrast and reinforcement to the human figures it contains. The image of evil in Blake's designs, consequently, is not an arbitrary emblem, or simply a devil with horns, but the sight of the human body surrendering its unique form and dissolving into a nonhuman landscape, as in many designs in the Lambeth books and the later prophecies where bodies take root in the ground or sprout bestial appendages.

The essential unity of Blake's composite art, then, lies in the convergence of each art form upon the single goal of affirming the centrality of the human form (as both imagination and body) in the structure of reality. Blake's art imitates neither an external world of objective "Nature" nor a purely internal world of subjective, arbitrary abstractions. Neither representationalism nor allegory satisfactorily defines the nature of his art. This latter point perhaps needs to be stressed most forcefully, since no one is about to mistake Blake for a Dutch painter, and since the allegorists generally have more to say about Blake than anyone else. Interpretation would indeed be easier if certain colors and certain abstract linear patterns had fixed, iconic meanings, but Blake would certainly be less interesting. The whole vitality of his art arises from his refusal to settle for the fixed, the emblematic, and the abstract, and from his decision to concentrate instead upon dramatizing the activity of the imagination in its encounter with reality. "Men think they can Copy Nature as I copy Imagination This they will find Impossible" (*PA*:E563). Blake's use of the word "imagination" as an object here has misled many critics into supposing that he has in mind the archetypal forms of some Platonic system as the objects of his copying. But imagination is not simply a product for Blake, a fixed body of well-defined forms; it is the *process* by which any symbolic form comes into being. When Blake says he "copies imagination," then, he means that he renders faithfully the activity of the mind as it alters the objects of perception: both the finished product and the process by which it comes into being are "imagination."

The consequences of this definition of Blake's art are perhaps more apparent in his poetry than in his art. Since Northrop Frye's *Fearful Symmetry* the nonallegorical nature of Blake's poetry has regularly been acknowledged, if not fully grasped. Nevertheless, the question of form in the major prophecies is still open. *Jerusalem* is still treated primarily as a quarry for Blakean "philosophy," not as a poetic structure with its own nondiscursive logic. When attempts are made to understand its form, they usually concentrate on one of the structural topoi to which Blake often alludes—the prophecy, the epic journey, the dream vision—rather than on Blake's own peculiar ideas about the principles of narrative form.[22] When these traditional ideas of form are recast in terms of Blake's own understanding of poetry as a critique of temporality and as a means of transcending it, we will see, I suspect, that *Milton* and *Jerusalem* have as much in common with *Tristram Shandy* as with *Paradise Lost*.

The basic groundwork for understanding Blake's pictorial symbolism remains to be done. Critics still tend either to content themselves with identification of subject matter (which assumes that the designs are mere illustrations) or to search for a fixed set of pictorial conventions. The attempts to formulate a color glossary, a left-right convention, or a set of denotative linear forms persist in spite of their continued failure to account for more than a very few pictures.[23] Blake makes clear, however, that no system of abstractions is to be found beyond or behind his art, and gives us instead a fairly straightforward set of general principles for understanding the generation of symbols by the dialectics in his compositions. His emphasis on the superiority of form and outline to light and color is well known yet misleading:

> The great and golden rule of art, as well as of life, is this: That the more distinct, sharp, and wiry the bounding line, the more perfect the work of art: and the less keen and sharp, the greater is the evidence of weak imitation.
>
> (*DC*:E540)

> The Beauty proper for sublime art is lineaments, or forms and features that are capable of being the receptacles of intellect;
>
> (*DC*:E535)

Blake's preference for linearity was probably in large measure a product of his early apprenticeship to James Basire, a master of the old-fashioned school of austerity in line engraving. The change in taste in late-eighteenth-century reproductive engraving to the softer lines and tonal emphasis of Woollett, Strange, and Bartolozzi[24] left Blake in possession of an increasingly unfashionable style, and probably accounts for some of his bitterness at the "painterly" schools. He was not isolated, however, in his preference for linearity. The neoclassical primitivism which Winckelmann had introduced was having its effect both in England and on the Continent. Diderot's hope for a reincarnation of Poussin was being fulfilled by David's meticulous historicism and sculpturely purity;[25] Flaxman and Cumberland, to name two of Blake's friends, were insisting on an even more radical purity and simplicity of outline.[26] The seeds of this preference for linearity had always been present in idealist conceptions of art,[27] and the theorists of the seventeenth and eighteenth centuries had consequently felt it necessary to defend the equal importance of color and light in painting long after it had been established in practice. Du Fresnoy, for instance, calls outline and color sisters, and defends the latter against the charge of prostituting outline: "And as this part, which we may call the utmost perfection of Painting, is a deceiving Beauty, but withall soothing and pleasing: So she has been accus'd of procuring Lovers for her Sister, and artfully engaging us to admire her. But so little have this Prostitution, these false Colours, and this Deceit, dishonour'd Painting, that on the contrary, they have only serv'd to set forth her praise."[28] The writers on *ut pictura poesis* likewise justified the use of color by comparing it to the expressive qualities of poetry: the relationship of color to outline is regularly equated with the relationship of verse to fable.[29] Color is seen by the Platonists as "art," a kind of cosmetic allurement to the "real meaning" which is contained in outline. To the Aristotelians, color permits a faithful imitation of nature's variety, and provides a verisimilitudinous setting for the general forms revealed by outline.

It is easy to say that Blake rejects these justifications of color, just as he rejects the Venetian "painterly" schools, and virtually makes a demonic trinity out of Rembrandt, Rubens, and Titian (see *DC*:E537–538). But it is not so clear what we should make of his actual use of color. We cannot say of Blake's designs, as we can of Flaxman's illustrations to Hesiod, Homer, and Dante, that they would gain nothing by the inclusion of color. Blake rarely produced an illustration to his own work without color, and black-and-white reproductions of his work are notoriously unsatisfying. Furthermore, to take at face value his claim that coloring is subservient to and determined by outline simply falsifies a good deal of his practice. In spite of his theoretical preference for clear outline and form, Blake often obscures his outlines with opaque pigments and heavy drapery.

The resolution of this apparent contradiction between theory and practice lies in a fuller understanding of the theory. The subservience of light to form is, for Blake, a visual equivalent of an ideal condition:[30]

> In Great Eternity, every particular Form gives forth or
>   Emanates
> Its own peculiar Light, & the Form is the Divine Vision
> And the Light is his Garment.
>
> *(J* 54:1–3)

The relation of form to light is defined as that of the Individual and his Emanation, or of consciousness and the external world which it projects. With the fall, however, consciousness becomes egotism (male will) and the external world becomes an independent Nature (female will). Form and light become, in this world, sexual principles working in opposition. The resolution of this opposition is attained by a procedure rather similar to the one we observed in the relation of text and design, a dialectic of contraries. When female nature, for instance, assumes an independent existence, it becomes "An outside shadowy surface super-added to the real Surface; / Which is unchangeable" (*J* 83:47–48): that is, color freed from outline and obscuring it is the visual equivalent of nature's obfuscating the imagination. The veil or garment is often used as a metaphor for this idea of color, and the disposition of drapery in Blake's pictures can be seen to follow the same principles as his treatment of color. Even though "Art & Science cannot exist but by Naked Beauty displayd" (*J* 32:49), Blake clothes many of his figures to exhibit their immersion into the fallen world of space and time. The frontispiece of *Jerusalem*, for instance, presents the clothed figure of Los-Blake entering the fallen world, the "Void outside of Existence, which if enterd into Englobes itself & becomes a Womb." The return of Los (*J* 97 {102}) from this world of Ulro or "Eternal Death" into the world of imagination (or true existence) displays his naked beauty. In the "Death's Door" illustration to Blair's *Grave* Blake similarly contrasts the entry into death (i.e., the fallen world) with the "awaking to Eternal life" by setting the clothed figure who enters the grave against the naked figure atop the grave. "The Drapery is formed alone by the Shape of the Naked" (Annotations to Reynolds: E639/K462) in theory, but in practice Blake often covers his figures (especially Urizen) with heavy, oppressive garments which obscure rather than reveal their lineaments.

It would be a mistake, however, to conclude that Blake's art is constructed simply on the principle that outline is "good" and the color or drapery which obscures it is "bad." The two compositional elements, like the two aspects of his composite art, engage in a dialectic that ranges from antagonism (when color becomes "An outside shadowy Surface" obscuring outline) to unity (when light serves as an aureole or halo around form), and all the stages of this dialectic are integral to the total vision. Blake provides us with a vocabulary for describing the range of his possible uses of form and light in the terms which he probably drew from his own experience as a painter. When man falls from his state of visionary perfection in Blake's myth, a universe or space must be created to set a limit to his fall: "The Divine Hand found two Limits: first of Opacity, then of Contraction" (*M* 13:20). These two limits are personified as Satan and Adam, and represent the lower boundaries of man's fall into spiritual darkness and the shrinking of his soul into an egotistic, self-enclosed organism. "But there is no Limit of Expansion! there is no Limit of Translucence" (*J* 42:35), except in the limitations of the painter's ability to create glowing images of bodily freedom. The applicability of these two terms to Blake's art is strongly suggested by his making them the basic structural principles of his art-city, Golgonooza, like Yeats's Byzantium, a regular metaphor for the total form of his artifices of eternity. (See *FZ* VIIa 87:E354.)

Two of Blake's most famous designs, the frontispiece to *Europe* and *Albion rose*, exemplify the contrast between contraction opacity and expansion / translucence. The figure captioned "Albion rose from where he labourd at the Mill with Slaves ..." {91} expands in a veritable sunburst of radiance. Blake wisely avoids trying to convey this radiance by direct means, such as mere whiteness, and instead depicts Albion as the light-source of all the colors of the spectrum; he serves as both the hub and spokes of a color-wheel. Just below Albion's knees the outer boundary of his radiance seems to expand into and dispel the darkness around his feet. The ground, which corresponds to the spiritual darkness and deformity from which he has risen, is presented as a riot of disorganized, opaque pigments, such as Blake used in depicting the seat of "that most outrageous demon," Newton.[31] Anthony Blunt has shown that this figure may have been derived from a diagram of the perfect human proportions in Scamozzi's *Idea dell'architettura universale*, in which the limbs of the figure are measured against a wheel with the center located at the navel.[32] Blake has moved the center of his figure down to the loins to enforce his idea that "The improvement of Sensual Enjoyment" (which corresponds, among other things, to the use of the erotic image, "Naked Beauty Display'd") is the proper means for reawakening the infinite in man. More important, Blake has freed his figure from the enclosing wheel, except perhaps for the token reminder of enclosure just below Albion's knees. If the design is indeed to be taken as employing a quotation from Scamozzi's treatise, it is certainly an ironic allusion, expressing Blake's conviction that his art is to be seen as a triumph over the tyranny of "mathematic form."

The contrasts with the frontispiece to *Europe* {8} need hardly be elaborated. Urizen is shown with his body bent and contracted into itself, enclosed in a circle. His one outward gesture is a thrust downward into the darkness to inscribe another circle on the abyss. Unlike Albion, who is the center of all the dynamism in his design, Urizen is the subject of the elements, as is revealed by the wind blowing his hair and the clouds closing in to obscure his radiance. If Albion is to be seen as bursting the circle of mathematical restriction, Urizen is the creator of that circle, and Blake's treatment of him must remind us of one of his most audacious epigrams:

> To God
> If you have formd a Circle to go into
> Go into it yourself & see how you would do
> (E508/K557)

The concepts of expansion and translucence, contraction and opacity are not to be placed in a simple equation with "good" and "evil," any more than outline and color can convey value in themselves. Blake always had a "contrary vision" in mind, in which any given symbolic organization could reverse its meaning. The act of creation, for instance, is a demonic act in that it encloses man in the "Mundane Shell," but it is, from another point of view, an act of mercy in that it prevents man from falling endlessly into the "Indefinite." In like manner, there is a sense in which contraction is a good, as in the state of Innocence when the mother creates a womblike space to protect the child. In *The Songs of Innocence* this aspect of contraction is given visual expression by "embracing" compositions. The space of the design is generally encircled in vines, or framed by an overarching arbor. Opacity also has its beneficial aspect, as can be seen in both text and design of *The Little Black Boy*, where it serves as a temporary protection from the overpowering translucence of God:

> And we are put on earth a little space,
> That we may learn to bear the beams of love,
> And these black bodies and this sun-burnt face
> Is but a cloud, and like a shady grove.

The protective functions of opacity and contraction in Innocence are transformed, of course, in *The Songs of Experience*. The tranquil, angel-guarded darkness of *Night* gives way to the threatening opacity of the "forests of the night" in Experience. The protective contraction of the arbor becomes the stark frame of a dead tree, the encircling vines become choking briars.

On the other hand, expansion and translucence are not unequivocally good. Blake often presents the figures of warfare or revolution as bright, expansive nudes. The figure of Orc, for instance, the personification of energy and rebellion against the circumscribed order of Urizen, is often depicted as a bright, youthful nude in an expansive pose. A good example of this kind of composition is plate 10 of *America* {38}, which shows Orc surrounded by flames, his arms extended in a kind of parody of the exultant expansion of *Albion rose*. Just two plates before this appears the well-known "Urizen on the Stone of Night," a design which has a completely different affective value from plate 10. But a close comparison of the two figures and the positions of their limbs reveals a point-for-point similarity. (See {36} and {38}.) The two pictures have, of course, completely opposite effects. Orc seems to rise and burst outward, the downward movement of his hands only providing thrust to his expansive movement, which is accentuated by his flaming hair and the exploding surroundings. The old man in his white robes, on the other hand, anatomically identical to Orc, produces the effect of contraction. His arms seem to merge into the stony background, pressed down by a great weight and weariness. The horizontal curves of the rocks reinforce the gravity which seems to push against and bend down the space of the picture. The juxtaposition of these two designs provides us with a visual equivalent of what Northrop Frye calls "the Orc cycle," the cyclical repetition of tyrannic repression and rebellious reaction. This essential identity of the rebel and his oppressor becomes the basis of Blake's critique of his own historical time, and in the later prophetic books a structural metaphor for time in the fallen world.

This identity of Orc and Urizen is also a further example of the interplay between abstraction and representation which is the basic mode of Blake's symbolism. The linear skeleton which permits us to identify these two figures has no particular meaning in itself: it does not "equal" Urizen or Orc, or the sum of their qualities. On the other hand, the particular representation of each of these mythical figures does not achieve its full symbolic status until we recognize that each is potentially the other, each is a metaphor for the other. Orc *is* Urizen, because the spirit of violent rebellion always degenerates into oppression when it has gained power. Urizen *is* Orc, because the tyrant inevitably begets the revolutionary reaction against his rule.[33] Neither abstraction nor representation, however, is permitted to become in itself the locus of this meaning. Significance is located in the dialectic between the permanence of outline and the mutability and momentary reality of color, just as in the poetry the continuity of consciousness is affirmed and realized in its ability persistently to give form to the changing manifestations of itself and the world it perceives.

The total design of the illuminated page affirms the identity of poem and picture by actualizing the continuity and interrelatedness of the most abstract linear patterns with the most representational forms. At the one extreme, visual form is constructed in accord with what is, from the point of view of the visual arts, a completely abstract, nonvisual system (language); at the other extreme, the picture exists to imitate the peculiarly visual aspects of experience. The word "Marriage" on the title page of *The Marriage of Heaven and Hell* affirms, appropriately enough, the actual marriage of these two concepts of form by serving as a bridge between the abstraction of typography and the mimesis of naturalistic representation. This may sound like an unnecessarily involved way of pointing out that Blake decorates his letters with foliage, as the medieval illuminators did. But the keystone of a complicated structure is always in the obvious, the inevitable place. The continuity which Blake manages to establish between the worlds of ideality and reality, subject and object in the dynamics of his two art forms is an integral part of the process of uniting these two forms into a single entity. And it is also the means by which the strange and wonderfully consistent world of his imagination manages to retain its own uncompromising otherness while establishing a continuity with and relevance to our own worlds.

NOTES

1. See also Blunt's full-length study, and his series of more specialized articles in *JWCI*, II (1938) and VI (1943). Other studies of interest include Geoffrey Keynes's *Blake Studies*, London, 1949, and the works cited in the present volume as Digby and Hagstrum. E. J. Rose has been issuing a series of articles based upon his "Mental Forms Creating: A Study of Blake's Thought and Symbols," Ph.D. diss., Univ. of Toronto, 1963–1964. The most recent specialized essay is Thomas Connolly and

George Levine, "Pictorial and Poetic Design in Two Songs of Innocence," *PMLA*, LXXXII (1967), 257–264.

2. Blunt, 2.

3. Letter to Dawson Turner, 9 June 1818 (K867).

4. An examination of the poetical contexts of the plates in *The Small Book of Designs* (conjectured by Keynes in his *Census* of Blake's illuminated books to be the plates which Blake sent to his friend) convinces me that at least 9 out of the 23 designs in this series have no apparent textual referent (pls. 1, 2, 5, 8, 9, 11–13, 18), and several others are quite ambiguous. One need only compare the specifications of content of these designs by Damon (*Philosophy*) and Keynes to see how unsure and contradictory the identifications are likely to be. Furthermore, the captions which Blake wrote at the bottoms of the plates in this series are in no instance taken from the poem that they illustrate.

5. In lieu of such a work, it is often useful to consult the Keynes-Wolf *Census* or Damon's *Philosophy*, exercising considerable caution.

6. For this general subject see Paul O. Kristeller, "The Modern System of the Arts, A Study in the History of Aesthetics," *Journal of the History of Ideas*, III (1951), 496–527.

7. Ralph Cohen, *The Art of Discrimination*, Berkeley, 1964.

8. Some of the more important studies of these ideas are Arthur Kenkel and Albrecht Shöne, eds., *Emblemata: Handbuch zur Sinnbildkunst des XVI und XVII Jahrhunderts*, Stuttgart, 1968; Robert J. Clements, *Picta Poesis: Literary and Humanistic Theory in Renaissance Emblem Books*, Rome, 1960; Jean Hagstrum, *The Sister Arts*, Chicago, 1958; and Rensselaer Lee, "'Ut Picture Poesis': The Humanistic Theory of Painting," *Art Bulletin*, XXII (1940), 197–269.

9. *Laocoön: An Essay on the Limits of Painting and Poetry*, 1766.

10. See, for example, the anonymous essay in *The Free Thinker*, no. 63 (22 October 1718; repr. London, 1722), II, 34–36, which argues that poetry is chiefly effective in time because mass publication permits it to endure. Painting, on the other hand, is ineffective in time because it is perishable, but conquers space because it leaps the language barrier.

11. See Mario Praz, *Studies in Seventeenth Century Imagery*, London, 1939, I, 155ff.

12. Giabattista Marino, *Dicerie sacre*, Vicenza, 1662, Essay I, Part ii, 52f. Quoted in Hagstrum, *The Sister Arts*, 94.

13. *The Sister Arts*, 96. I owe several of the following examples to Hagstrum and Lee.

14. *Iconologia*, Padua, 1618, 416; translated in Hagstrum, 94.

15. *The Plain Dealer*, II, no. 60 (London, 1730).

16. Letters to Thomas Butts, 6 July 1803, and Dr. Trusler, 23 August 1799 (K825, 793).

17. It has been suggested by John E. Grant that the title page "illustrates" the text of *MHH* 24, which describes the dialogue of an angel and devil, and the conversion of the former into the latter. A considerable number of qualifications would have to accompany this view of the relationship: 1) the textual devil and angel are males, while the pictured figures are female; 2) the text describes a conversation followed by a self-immolation, while the design depicts a sexual encounter; 3) the other details of the design do not seem to refer to the text of plate 24. An accurate understanding of the relationship between the design and any textual echoes of its details must take into account, it seems to me, the complex transformations involved in transposing the elements of one to the other. One could argue, for instance, that self-immolation and sexuality are a kind of natural metaphor, and certainly a very Blakean one; yet this would still only scratch the surface of the complex metaphorical layers that would be involved in any equation of *MHH* 1 with *MHH* 24.

J.E.G.: I agree that some of these reservations need to be borne in mind lest one assume, as Damon does, that the episode depicted is intended as an "illustration" in the sense of a literal depiction of the last Memorable Fancy. The hazards of descriptive generalizations based on a single copy, however, need also to be guarded against: the round buttocks and long hair on the figure at the left in copy F (Blake Trust facsimile) make the figure seem female, the more svelte buttocks in copy H (Dent facsimile) could easily be those of a male; hair length is not a safe guide; and Blake often chose not to depict the genitalia of indubitably male figures. One could argue that the pictured "Devil" and "Angel" are both androgynes, but it seems simplest to treat them as male and female respectively, as I have done in my discussion of the page in "Two Flowers in the Garden of Experience," in Rosenfeld, *Essays for Damon*, 363–364. For one thing, the word "Marriage" in the title and these embracing figures on the same page (though the page contains other details, since it is designed for viewers, not just readers) require readers to concern themselves with implications that make sense of the conversion of the Angel at the end of the poem. This conversion is described as his encountering "a Devil in a flame of fire" (cf. the left-hand figure in flames in the title page) and, from where he sits "on a cloud" (cf. the right-hand figure), stretching "out his arms embracing the flame of fire"—upon which "he was consumed and arose as Elijah," who, we are reminded later, "comprehends all the Prophetic Characters" (*VLJ* 83). To summarize this as "self-immolation" is to ignore the transparent and traditional sexual symbolism and to forget there was a Devil in this flame. Were not Blake's title and title page designed to make the human presence of a long-haired Devil in the flame embarrassingly obvious to angelic readers? One must, so to speak, take a Black Panther to lunch before he is fit to enter the kingdom of prophecy.

Those who find anything but the expression of this principle anachronistic are invited to observe several facts. The first is that in copy F, the Blake Trust facsimile, the figure at the right is colored dark brown, quite dark enough to be counted as "black" either in the eighteenth century or now, especially when it is contrasted with the very pinkish "white" figure at the left. It would be more convenient for the reader if this color symbolism were reversed so that the infernal character were black, but the viewer will find the further ironies of the actual coloration both intelligible and satisfying. He will also observe that Blake did not employ this color symbolism in most versions of the book, but understand that this does not negate the significance in copies where he did so.

If a contemporary racist, such as Gillray, had seen the title page of copy F, he might have concluded that Blake was advocating miscegenation. But two other considerations will assist the appreciation of Blake's point in all versions of this design. Although the relationships indicated in the background are more intimate, the central consummation depicted is clearly no more than a kiss. In the text of *MHH* 24 Blake neglects to mention the human form in the flame embraced by the Angel—and thus prevents the conversion of angelic character from seeming easy. In the introduction to this section, in plate 22, Blake declares that the writings of Dante are infinitely more informative than those of the angelic Swedenborg; perhaps Blake had already read that episode in the *Purgatorio* where Dante, like all pilgrims to eternity, must pass through the circumambient fire of love to return, like Adam into paradise, to where Beatrice is.

There have been many accounts of what *The Marriage of Heaven and Hell* is about. I say it is about the education of the Prophetic Character. Blake is committed to showing how much pain and dislocation such an education demands. Though he was honest about the magnitude of the task, he was glad to join with Moses and Milton in praying that all the Lord's people become prophets.

18. The reclining figure is clearly a woman in copy C (Morgan Library) and in copy D and the Trianon Press facsimile of this copy; the instrument held by the kneeling figure is only suggestively etched— probably a flute or shepherd's pipe, or it could be a lyre.

19. See ch. 9, "The Unity of Action," in Lee's "'Ut Pictura Poesis.'"

20. See Rosenblum, *Transformations*, 158, for an account of Blake's "regression" from the illusionistic style and an intriguing explanation of its relation to other primitivistic experiments in the arts.

21. Hogarth's interiors provide a striking example of conscious use of this technique. See particularly Ronald Paulson's *"The Harlot's Progress* and the Tradition of History Painting," *Eighteenth Century Studies*, I (1967–1968), 73. For an explanation of the use of a similar device in landscape painting, see Jeffrey Eicholz, "William Kent's Career as a Literary Illustrator," *BNYPL*, LXX (1966), 620–646.

22. Two exemplary studies of *Jerusalem* are E. J. Rose, "The Structure of Blake's Jerusalem," *Bucknell Review*, XI (1963), 35–54, and Karl Kiralis, "The Theme and Structure of Blake's Jerusalem," *ELH*, XXIII (1956), 127–143. Both critics try to construct a linear, sequential model for *Jerusalem*, and both fall short. It is interesting to note, however, that the two studies are about equally accurate in what they do say about the progressions in the poem, and yet they say diametrically opposite things. Kiralis sees the structure as analogous to the stages in human growth; Rose sees it as precisely the reverse, a journey backward in time. (See Lesnick's essay, pp. 391ff.)

23. Attempts to impose a lateral convention are quite persistent in spite of their inadequacies. E.J. Rose ("Visionary Forms Dramatic: Grammatical and Iconographical Movement in Blake's Designs and Verse," *Criticism*, VIII [1966], 111–125), and Claudette Kemper ("The Interlinear Drawings in Blake's Jerusalem," *BNYPL*, LXIV [1960], 588–594) propose with equal assurance diametrically opposed

interpretations of the meanings of right and left in Jerusalem. The point is, of course, that neither right nor left has any fixed meaning but that pictorial reversals and inversions, in particular and local contexts, may produce meaning.

24. Arthur M. Hind, *A History of Engraving and Etching*, London, 1928; rev. 1963, 204–206, 209.

25. See Jean Seznec, "Diderot and Historical Painting," in *Aspects of the Eighteenth Century*, ed. E.R. Wasserman, Baltimore, 1965, 139.

26. Blake did all the engravings from Flaxman's drawings for *Compositions from the Works Days and Theogony of Hesiod*, London, 1817, and a few for *The Iliad of Homer*, London, 1805. He also taught Cumberland how to engrave, and executed his designs for *Thoughts* on *Outline*, London, 1796.

27. See Dora and Irwin Panofsky, *Pandora's Box*, New York, 1956, 91.

28. *The Art of Painting*, tr. John Dryden, 2nd edn. London, 1716; excerpts in *A Documentary History of Art*, ed. Elizabeth Holt, New York, 1958, 170.

29. See Dryden's preface, "A Parallel of Poetry and Painting," to Du Fresnoy's *De Arte Graphica*, in *The Essays of John Dryden*, ed. W. P. Ker (London, 1900), ii, 147f. See also Abbé Batteaux, *Les Beaux Arts reduits à un même principe*, Paris, 1746, 247, for the equation of "desseing" with "fable" and "coloris" with "versification."

30. In the discussion which follows I will not distinguish rigorously between the terms "color" and "light," and "outline" and "form." Blake uses the terms almost interchangeably, and sees them as completely interdependent in theory.

31. Reproduced in Blunt, pl. 30c.

32. "Blake's Glad Day," *JWCI*, VI (1948), 225–227.

33. David Erdman has shown in this volume ("*America*: New Expanses") that Blake does not express this vision of the Orc cycle in the text of *America*, and suggests that he did not develop this concept of the cycle until the 1800s. My interpretation, therefore, may be subject to considerable qualification, although, as we have seen elsewhere, Blake was certainly capable of saying things in his designs which he never expressed in the accompanying text. The significant point, nevertheless, is the method by which meaningful interplay between outline and color is established in related designs. It may be an overstatement to say that "Orc is Urizen" in the context of these two plates, but it is certainly

accurate to note that some kind of metaphorical relationship has been created by the similarities of the two designs.

Chronology

1757	Born in London, 28 November.
1767	Father sends him to Henry Par's drawing school in the Strand.
1768	Begins writing *Poetical Sketches*.
1771	Becomes an apprentice of Basire the engraver.
1779	Leaves Basire and enters the Royal Academy.
1780	Gordon Riots in London (June), in which Blake may have participated; arrested on suspicion of spying during sketching trip on the River Medway.
1782	50 copies of *Poetical Sketches* printed; becomes a freelance engraver; marries Catherine Boucher on 18 August.
1783	Blake's father dies in July.
1784	Opens a print shop with James Parker at 27 Broad Street; begins writing *An Island in the Moon* (c. 1784–85).
1787	Brother Robert dies at age 19; in a vision, Robert shows Blake a new method of engraving, relief etching.
1788	*All Religions Are One* and *There Is No Natural Religion*, the first of his illuminated works, published.
1789	*Songs of Innocence* published; begins *The Book of Thel*; writes *Tiriel*.

1790	*Marriage of Heaven and Hell* published.
1791	*The French Revolution* type set; mother dies; illustrates Mary Wollstonecraft's *Original Stories from Real Life*.
1793	*America: A Prophecy* published; *Visions of the Daughters of Albion* published; *For Children: The Gates of Paradise* published. Engraves *Albion Rose*.
1794	*Songs of Innocence and of Experience* published; *The First Book of Urizen* published.
1795	*The Song of Los The Book of Ahania*, *The Book of Los* published; produces 12 large color-printed drawings; works on 537 water color illustrations for Edward Young's *Night Thoughts*.
1796	Begins writing *Vala, or The Four Zoas*.
1797	Begins set of 116 water color illustrations to the poems of Thomas Gray for John Flaxman; Young's *Night Thoughts* published with 43 plates engraved by Blake after his own designs.
1800	Moves to Felpham in Sussex to work for patron William Hayley.
1801	Produces eight water color illustrations of Milton's *Comus* for the Rev. Joseph Thomas.
1803	Charged with high treason (based on the testimony of an inebriated soldier) and put on trial at Chichester; quarrels with Hayley and returns to London.
1804	Is acquitted on treason charges; his exhibition at the Royal Academy fails to attract any significant interest. Begins work on *Milton a Poem* and *Jerusalem The Emanation of the Giant Albion*.
1805	Begins illustrations for Blair's *The Grave*, to be published by Robert Cromek; produces 19 water color illustrations of the *Book of Job* for Thomas Butts.
1809	Exhibits 16 paintings at 28 Broad Street, accompanied by a *Descriptive Catalogue* defending his theory and practice.

1810	Begins to suffer bouts of severe depression which last until 1817.
1817	*Hesiod* is published.
1818	Meets John Linnell; begins sketching "Visionary Heads" for John Varley.
1820	First Copy of *Jerusalem* printed; publishes *For the Sexes: The Gates of Paradise*.
1821	Virgil's *Pastorals*, edited by Robert John Thornton, published with wood engravings by Blake.
1822	Publishes *The Ghost of Abel* and *On Homer's Poetry* and *On Virgil*.
1824	Begins illustrations to Dante's *Divine Comedy* and Bunyan's *Pilgrim's Progress*.
1826	Publishes 21 engraved *Illustrations of the Book of Job*; produces *Laocoön*; begins Genesis Manuscript.
1827	12 August, dies of complications from gallstones. Is buried in an unmarked grave at Bunhill Fields.

Works by William Blake

Poetical Sketches, 1768–1783

An Island in the Moon, 1784

There Is No Natural Religion, 1788

All Religions Are One, 1788

Tiriel, 1788–1789

Songs of Innocence, 1789

Book of Thel, 1789

The Marriage of Heaven and Hell, 1790

The French Revolution, Book I, 1791

Visions of the Daughters of Albion, 1793

For Children: The Gates of Paradise, 1793

America: A Prophecy, 1793

Songs of Experience, 1794

Europe: A Prophecy, 1794

The First Book of Urizen, 1794

The Song of Los, 1795

The Book of Los, 1795

The Book of Ahania, 1795

The Four Zoas, 1797–1807

Milton, 1804–1808

A Descriptive Catalogue, 1809
Jerusalem: The Emanation of the Giant Albion, 1804–1820
The Ghost of Abel, 1822

Works about William Blake

Ackroyd, Peter. *Blake*. New York, NY: Knopf, 1996.

Adams, Hazard. *William Blake: A Reading of the Shorter Poems*. Seattle, WA: University of Washington Press, 1963.

Altizer, Thomas J.J. *The New Apocalypse: The Radical Christian Vision of William Blake*. East Lansing, MI: Michigan State University Press, 1967.

Ault, Donald. *Visionary Physics: Blake's Response to Newton*. Chicago, IL: University of Chicago Press, 1974.

Bentley, G.E., Jr. *The Stranger from Paradise: A Biography of William Blake*. New Haven, CT: Yale University Press, 2001.

Bindman, David. *Blake as an Artist*. New York, NY: Dutton, 1977.

Blake, William. *Blake's Poetry and Designs*. Mary Lynn Johnson and John E. Grant, ed. New York, NY: W.W. Norton, 1979.

————. *Blake: Complete Writings with Variant Readings*. 3rd ed. Geoffrey Keynes, ed. Oxford, UK: Oxford University Press, 1979.

Bloom, Harold, ed. *William Blake* (Modern Critical Views). Philadelphia, PA: Chelsea House Publishers, 1985.

Bloom, Harold. *Blake's Apocalypse*. Ithaca, NY: Cornell University Press, 1970.

Bronowski, J. *William Blake and the Age of Revolution*. New York, NY: Harper & Row, 1965.

Creehan, Stewart. "William Blake." *The Penguin History of Literature:*

The Romantic Period. David B. Pirie, ed. New York, NY: Penguin, 1994. 117–50.

Damon, S. Foster. *A Blake Dictionary: The Ideas and Symbols of William Blake.* Revised edition. Hanover, NH: University Press of New England, 1988.

———. *William Blake: His Philosophy and Symbols.* London, UK: Dawsons of Pall Mall, 1969.

Damrosch, Leopold, Jr. *Symbol and Truth in Blake's Myth.* Princeton, NJ: Princeton University Press, 1980.

Davies, Mark. *Blake's Milton Designs: The Dynamics of Meaning.* West Cornwall, CT: Locust Hill, 1993.

De Luca, Vincent Arthur. *Words of Eternity: Blake and the Poetics of the Sublime.* Princeton, NJ: Princeton University Press, 1991.

Digby, George Wingfield. *Symbol and Image in William Blake.* Oxford, UK: Clarendon, 1957.

Eaves, Morris. *The Cambridge Companion to William Blake.* Cambridge, UK: Cambridge University Press, 2003.

———. *William Blake's Theory of Art.* Princeton, NJ: Princeton University Press, 1982

Erdman, David. V., *The Complete Poetry andProse of William Blake.* Ed., with commentary by Harold Bloom. Berkeley, CA: University of California Press, 1988.

———. *Blake: Prophet against Empire.* 3rd ed. New York, NY: Dover, 1977.

Erdman David V., et al., eds. *A Concordance to the Writings of William Blake.* Ithaca, NY: Cornell University Press, 1967.

Essick, Robert N. *William Blake, Printmaker.* Princeton, NJ: Princeton University Press, 1980.

Fisher, Peter F. *The Valley of Vision: Blake as Prophet and Revolutionary.* Northrop Frye, ed. Toronto, CA: University of Toronto Press, 1961.

Frosch, Thomas R. *The Awakening of the Albion: The Renovation of the Body in the Poetry of William Blake.* Ithaca, NY: Cornell University Press, 1974.

Frye, Northrop. "Blake's Treatment of the Archetype." *English Institute*

Essays: 1950. Alan S. Downer, ed. New York, NY: Columbia University Press, 1951. 170–96.

———. *Fearful Symmetry: A Study of William Blake.* Princeton, NJ: Princeton University Press, 1947.

Gilchrist, Alexander. *The Life of William Blake.* W. Graham Robertson, ed. Mineola, NY: Dover, 1998.

Gleckner, Robert F. *The Piper and The Bard: A Study of William Blake.* Detroit, MI: Wayne State University Press, 1960.

Hagstrum, Jean H. *William Blake: Poet and Painter.* Chicago: University of Chicago Press, 1964.

Heppner, Christopher. *Reading Blake's Designs.* Cambridge, UK: Cambridge University Press, 1995.

Hilton, Nelson, ed. *Essential Articles for the Study of William Blake, 1970–1984.* Hamden, CT: Archon Books, 1986.

Keynes, Geoffrey, ed. *Blake Studies: Essays on His Life and Work.* 2nd ed. Oxford, UK: Clarendon, 1971.

Keynes, Geoffrey, ed. *William Blake: Poet, Printer, Prophet: A Study of the Illuminated Books.* New York, NY: Orion, 1964.

Klonsky, Milton. *William Blake: The Seer and His Visions.* New York, NY: Harmony Books, 1977.

Makdisi, Saree. *William Blake and the Impossible History of the 1790s.* Chicago, IL: University of Chicago Press, 2003.

Mee, Jon. *Dangerous Enthusiasm. William Blake and the Culture of Radicalism in the 1790s.* Oxford, UK: Clarendon Press, 1992.

Mellor, Anne K. *Blake's Human Form Divine.* Berkeley, CA; University of California Press, 1974.

Miner, Paul. "William Blake's Divine Analogy." *Criticism* 3 (1961): 46–61.

Mitchell, W.J.T. *Blake's Composite Art.* Princeton, NJ: Princeton University Press, 1978.

———. "Visible Language: Blake's Wond'rous Art of Writing." *Romanticism and Contemporary Criticism.* Morris Eaves and Michael Fischer, ed. Ithaca, NY: Cornell University Press, 1986. 46–95.

Moskal, Jeanne. *Blake, Ethics and Forgiveness.* Tuscaloosa, AL: University of Alabama Press, 1994.

Murry, John Middleton. *William Blake.* New York, NY: McGraw-Hill, 1964.

Nurmi, Martin K. *William Blake.* London, UK: Hutchinson, 1975.

Ostriker, Alicia. *Vision and Verse in William Blake.* Madison, WI: University of Wisconsin Press, 1965.

Otto, Peter. *Constructive Vision and Visionary Deconstruction: Los, Eternity, and the Productions of Time in the Later Poetry of William Blake.* Oxford, UK: Clarendon Press, 1991.

Paley, Morton D. *Energy and the Imagination: A Study of the Development of Blake's Thought.* Oxford, UK: Clarendon, 1970.

———. *William Blake.* New York, NY: Dutton, 1978.

Percival, Milton O. *William Blake's Circle of Destiny.* New York, NY: Columbia University Press, 1938.

Peterfreund, Stuart. *William Blake in a Newtonian World: Essays on Literature as Art and Science.* Norman, OK: University of Oklahoma Press, 1998.

Pierce, John B. *The Wond'rous Art: William Blake and Writing.* Madison, NJ: Fairleigh Dickinson University Press, 2003.

Phillips, Michael, ed. *Interpreting Blake.* Cambridge: Cambridge University Press, 1978.

Pinto, Vivian de Sola, ed. *The Divine Vision: Studies in the Poetry and Art of William Blake.* London, UK: Gollancz, 1957.

Raine, Kathleen. *Blake and Tradition.* Bollingen Series XXV. Princeton, NJ: Princeton University Press, 1968.

———. *Golgonooza, City of Imagination: Last Studies in William Blake.* Hudson, NY: Lindisfarne Press, 1991.

Rose, Edward J. "Blake's Metaphorical States." *Blake Studies* 4 (1971): 9–31.

———. "Good-bye to Orc and All That." *Blake Studies* 4 (1972): 135–151.

———. "The Meaning of Los." *Blake Newsletter* 1.3 (1967): 10–11.

Rosenfeld, Alvin H., ed. *William Blake: Essays for S. Foster Damon.* Providence, RI: Brown University Press, 1969.

Rothenberg, Molly Anne. *Rethinking Blake's Textuality.* Columbia, MO: University of Missouri Press, 1993.

Schorer, Mark. *William Blake: The Politics of Vision*. New York, NY: Anchor, 1959.

Tannenbaum, Leslie. *Biblical Translations in Blake's Early Prophecies: The Great Code of Art*. Princeton, NJ: Princeton University Press, 1982.

Thompson, E.P. *Witness Against the Beast: William Blake and the Moral Law*. Cambridge, UK: Cambridge University Press, 1993.

Viscomi, Joseph. *Blake and the Idea of the Book*. Princeton, NJ: Princeton University Press, 1993.

Warner, Janet. *Blake and the Language of Art*. Montreal: McGill-Queen's University Press, 1984.

Wilkie, Brian, and Mary Lynn Johnson. *Blake's* Four Zoas: *The Design of a Dream*. Cambridge, MA: Harvard University Press, 1978.

Wilson, Mona. *The Life of William Blake*. 3rd ed. Oxford, UK: Oxford University Press, 1971.

Wittreich, Joseph Anthony Jr. *Angel of Apocalypse: Blake's Idea of Milton*. Madison, WI: University of Wisconsin Press, 1975.

WEBSITES

Blake Digital TextProject
virtual.park.uga.edu/wblake/home1.html

The Blake List
www.albion.com/blake/

Web Museum: Blake, William
www.ibiblio.org/wm/paint/auth/blake/

William Blake—The Academy of American Poets
www.poets.org/poets/poets.cfm?45442B7C000C07040E

William Blake Archive
www.blakearchive.org/

William Blake Online
www.tate.org.uk/britain/exhibitions/blakeinteractive/

William Blake –Wikipedia
en.wikipedia.org/wiki/William_Blake

Contributors

HAROLD BLOOM is Sterling Professor of the Humanities at Yale University. He is the author of over 20 books, including *Shelley's Mythmaking* (1959), *The Visionary Company* (1961), *Blake's Apocalypse* (1963), *Yeats* (1970), *A Map of Misreading* (1975), *Kabbalah and Criticism* (1975), *Agon: Toward a Theory of Revisionism* (1982), *The American Religion* (1992), *The Western Canon* (1994), and *Omens of Millennium: The Gnosis of Angels, Dreams, and Resurrection* (1996). *The Anxiety of Influence* (1973) sets forth Professor Bloom's provocative theory of the literary relationships between the great writers and their predecessors. His most recent books include *Shakespeare: The Invention of the Human* (1998), a 1998 National Book Award finalist, *How to Read and Why* (2000), *Genius: A Mosaic of One Hundred Exemplary Creative Minds* (2002), *Hamlet: Poem Unlimited* (2003), and *Where Shall Wisdom be Found* (2004). In 1999, Professor Bloom received the prestigious American Academy of Arts and Letters Gold Medal for Criticism, and in 2002 he received the Catalonia International Prize.

NEIL HEIMS is a freelance writer, editor, and researcher. He has a Ph.D. in English from the City University of New York. He has written on a number of authors including Albert Camus, Arthur Miller, John Milton, and J.R.R. Tolkien.

HEATHER DUBNICK has received her Ph.D. in Spanish Literature from Johns Hopkins University and her MS in Library and Information

Science from Simmons College. She has published papers on Borges in *Romance Notes* and *Literary Texts and the Arts: Interdisciplinary Perspectives* (2003). She is Co-Founder and Principal, Ampersand Enterprises.

ROBERT F. GLECKNER was Professor of English at Duke University. Among his many publications are *Piper & the Bard: A Study of William Blake* (1959); *Byron and the Ruins of Paradise* (1967); *Poetical Works of Byron* (1975); *Blakes Prelude: "Poetical Sketches"* (1982); and *Blake and Spenser* (1985).

NORTHROP FRYE, preeminent among Canadian literary critics, was professor of English at University of Toronto (Victoria College) and later the chancellor at Victoria University. Of his many books, some of the best known are *Fearful Symmetry: A Study of William Blake*; *Anatomy of Criticism*; *The Well-Tempered Critic*; *T.S. Eliot, Fables of Identity*; and *The Great Code*.

W.J.T. MITCHELL is Professor of English and Art History at the University of Chicago where he is editor of the interdisciplinary journal, *Critical Inquiry*. Among his publications are *The Last Dinosaur Book: The Life and Times of a Cultural Icon* (1998); *Picture Theory* (1994); *Art and the Public Sphere* (1993); *Landscape and Power* (1992); *Iconology* (1987); *The Language of Images* (1980); *On Narrative* (1981); and *The Politics of Interpretation* (1984).

INDEX